125 – THE ENDURING ICON

125 Group

AMBERLEY

Front cover: Freshly repainted East Midlands Trains power car No. 43048 *TCB Miller MBE* shows the application of a complex modern livery scheme on the classic lines of the famous InterCity 125 nose cone. This was the first power car to be turned out in this colour scheme and is seen at Neville Depot, Leeds, on 30 April 2008 on the occasion of the power car being named after the man who led the design team that created the HST. The HST remains the standard by which other trains are judged. (John Tattersall)

First published 2018

Amberley Publishing
The Hill, Stroud
Gloucestershire, GL5 4EP

www.amberley-books.com

ISBN 978 1 4456 7859 7 (print)
ISBN 978 1 4456 7860 3 (ebook)

British Library Cataloguing in Publication Data.
A catalogue record for this book is available from the British Library.

Origination by Amberley Publishing.
Printed in the UK.

Contents

Foreword 5

Chapter 1: This is the Age of the Train 6

Chapter 2: The Train that Means Business 19

Chapter 3: New Looks, New Names, New Directions 32

Chapter 4: 125s Beyond the Main Line 67

Chapter 5: Valenta, a Tough Act to Follow 82

Chapter 6: Project Miller; Prototype Metamorphosis 89

Foreword

Good fortune led to my involvement with the High Speed Train (HST), when British Rail approached my firm to produce a livery for the new train and I took it upon myself to also come up with an improved shape. For the first time in train design we adopted measured aerodynamics, using the wind tunnel at Imperial College to test our models and evolve the best shape. When the day came to show BR our livery, we took along the new model and photographs of smoke trails in the wind tunnel. They listened to our arguments and approved the new design for what became known as the Prototype HST, built with buffers and based upon one person driving, who would be looking out of a small armoured windscreen.

Main line testing was successful but crucially the trade unions insisted on two driving positions. So we set about coming up with a new design, making and testing new models, but couldn't match the aerodynamics of the prototype, which benefitted from very shallow curved side pillars. By making the windscreen wider for two drivers, the side pillars had to be more acute, and therefore less aerodynamic. We spent great effort trying to make the buffers aerodynamic because we knew from wind tunnel tests these had a big impact. BR came back with the revelation that buffers would not be needed for the shunting role of a typical 'railway engine'. By removing them, the front rake of the cab could be much longer and therefore more aerodynamic. This was elementary and the result was the production power car – the InterCity 125.

This distinctive shape is only a small part of the product, brought to life by hundreds of engineers of every variety who made my fantasy into these iconic powerful movers of millions. Of all my work, I am most proud of the HST. This book charts its history, affectionately followed and documented by the enthusiast community. I am honoured to be titular head of 125 Group – that devoted bunch – whose thousands of unpaid hours brought No. 41001 back to life, and whose determination will hopefully see an InterCity 125 preserved for future generations.

Sir Kenneth Grange

Sir Kenneth Grange is the eminent industrial designer who designed everything from cameras and food mixers to taxis and the iconic InterCity 125 power car cab shape. We are extremely proud to have Sir Kenneth Grange as the honorary president of 125 Group.

Chapter 1

This is the Age of the Train

The outline design emerged from within British Rail's (BR) engineering department in 1969. It required an express passenger train of lightweight construction, powered by a diesel locomotive at either end of a rake of intermediate coaches, and would be capable of 125 mph with the braking ability to stop within the signal spacing of the prevailing railway environment. The growing realisation that the flagship Advanced Passenger Train project would not deliver a train capable of squadron service until well into the next decade exposed the need for a stop gap; BR needed to reduce journey times on intercity routes in answer to competition from the growing road network. A high-speed diesel train (HSDT) founded on proven and available railway technology became an attractive option and funding for the construction of the prototype was secured in 1970. Detailed design and construction work was overseen by BR's Traction and Rolling Stock Design Department under the auspices of its chief, Terry Miller.

When the completed power cars and trailers emerged respectively from Crewe and Derby Litchurch Lane Works, they were designated and numbered as conventional locomotives and coaching stock. Power cars Nos 41001/2, completed in 1972, sat on Bo-Bo bogies with power provided by a Paxman Valenta engine rated at 2,250 hp. The latest incarnation of BR's express passenger coach, designated Mark 3, was 75 feet 4 inches in length, was of lightweight steel construction, double glazed and air conditioned, and came with the promise of improved comfort and ride quality. The prototype was initially based at Neville Hill, with a trial running between Leeds, Newcastle and Edinburgh commencing in early 1973. The set operated in numerous configurations, with research vehicles often in situ. On 12 June 1973, Nos 41001/2 set a diesel world speed record with a recorded maximum of 143.2 mph on a run from York to Darlington. After nearly 100,000 miles of test running the set returned to works in June 1974 for overhaul. During the works visit the prototype and its constituent vehicles were reclassified as Class 252 multiple unit stock. The power cars and trailers were renumbered in the 4xxxx coaching stock series, and the complete set became No. 252001. BR's intention to operate them as fixed formation trains was further confirmed by the fitting of an auxiliary alternator to No. 43000 (ex-No. 41001) to provide 415 V three-phase AC current to power the trailers' lighting, air conditioning and catering equipment; this system of powering the auxiliaries on the production builds made HST vehicles incompatible with conventional locomotives and coaching stock but eliminated the need for heavy and unreliable Motor Alternator equipment. On completion of its overhaul, No. 252001 was transferred to the Western Region (WR) at Old Oak Common for further testing and finally, from May 1975, regular passenger working on the London–Bristol route.

Operation of the prototype had been hampered by trade union resistance to the cab layout of a single centrally positioned driver's seat, so changes were needed for the production power cars. These were most noticeable on the front end, which was completely restyled by design consultant Kenneth Grange. Aerodynamic wind tunnel testing led to his evolution of a more sharply sloping front with a single broad glass windscreen. A flush appearance was aided by the absence of conventional buffer gear and the warning horns and lights were accommodated together in a neat symmetrical arrangement embedded below the cab windscreen. Although the coaches were to carry standard BR blue and grey livery, the power car livery developed by Grange in conjunction with the design panel was to be black and yellow, changing over to the coach livery around the guard's compartment. Early in 1976 it was decided that standard BR blue was more suitable than black and the few initial power cars finished in the original scheme were swiftly repainted. On both versions silver InterCity 125 lettering and the BR double arrow symbol appeared high up on the power car bodysides. The High Speed Train was now to be marketed to the public as InterCity 125 (IC125), with the legend '125' appearing on timetables indicating operation by the new train.

Construction of production IC125 vehicles began in 1975 after the government authorised orders for twenty-seven seven-car sets, Nos 253001–027, power cars Nos W43002–55 for the London–Bristol/South Wales route and thirty-two eight-car sets, Nos 254001–032 (Nos E43056–85, Nos SC43086–95, Nos E43096–119), for the London–Leeds/Newcastle/Edinburgh services, operated by the Eastern Region (ER) and Scottish Region (ScR). The submissions also made provision for the construction of specialist IC125 depots on the WR at Old Oak Common (London) and St Philips Marsh (Bristol) and on the ER/ScR at Bounds Green (London), Neville Hill (Leeds), Heaton (Newcastle) and Craigentinny (Edinburgh). Regions were required to undertake improvements to the railway infrastructure at various locations to bring it up to modern standards and maximise the potential for high-speed running. Deliveries to the WR commenced in March 1976, and as further sets arrived an intensive testing and crew training programme began in late April, with passenger operation on existing timings beginning during the summer. The introduction of a limited number of sets into regular passenger service in accelerated 125 mph timings on 4 October 1976 marked the beginning of the IC125 era. Deliveries of new sets continued through 1977 and utilisation was gradually stepped up with the full service on the WR effective from October 1977. The introduction of Nos 253001–027 was not without its problems. As diagrammed mileage was increased in 1977, a number of technical difficulties emerged with power units, turbochargers and bogies. Availability hovered around 70 per cent and a concerted effort on the part of BR's engineering department together with close cooperation from external suppliers was required to address these early teething problems.

As a result of service experience gained on the WR, the introduction of IC125s to the East Coast Main Line (ECML) was much easier from a maintenance perspective. Deliveries that had begun with Nos E43056/57 in July 1977 progressed steadily, and from May 1978 six diagrams became operational on the core route. By October 1978 enough sets were in traffic to enable Leeds and Aberdeen to join the InterCity 125 network. Completion of the order for Nos 254001–032 in May 1979 enabled the introduction of full working on the ECML. Extension of IC125 operation to the West of England, for which fourteen Class 253 sets had been ordered, was to prove difficult. Unlike their predecessors, which had Brush equipment, the power cars for Nos 253028–041 (Nos 43125–152 and spare No. 43124) were fitted with traction motors supplied by GEC. When they entered traffic from June 1979 onwards it became evident that they were unreliable and barely fit for purpose. Power car deliveries were halted completely by BR in 1980 until GEC accepted responsibility and addressed the problem. Partial IC125 working between Paddington, Plymouth and Penzance commenced in October 1979 but plans to implement the full service from May 1980 had to be deferred until June 1981.

While the introduction of IC125s had presented many challenges, their commercial success was not in doubt. Growth in passenger numbers on the routes where they were employed continued to rise significantly into the late 1970s, particularly on the ECML, where overcrowding on many services had become an issue. In late 1979, in order to improve capacity and to extend IC125 working on the Eastern Region, BR sought to build seven additional Class 254 sets but only received authorisation for four. The political and economic climate had changed with a new government in power less inclined to commit public funds to the railway and the beginnings of deep recession. As a consequence, BR embarked on a review of its IC125 deployment strategy. This resulted in the decision to transfer two WR sets to the ECML in 1981, which in effect led to the curtailment of the building of No. 253041 and the transfer of No. 253027 (Nos 43054/55) to the ER in October 1981.

The construction of eighteen sets for North East–South West (NE–SW) services authorised in 1978 was meant to follow the West of England batch. The need of the ECML was so pressing that the first power cars from this batch (Nos 43153–162) were delivered to the ER in early 1981. With trailer construction now ahead of power cars, additional sets Nos 254033–037 were formed. Deliveries for sets Nos 253041–058 (Nos 43163–43198) commenced in the summer of 1981. The NE–SW sets were to differ from their Class 253 counterparts in having only one first-class and five second-class trailers together with a single catering car. A limited IC125 service on the 'Heartline' Cross Country axis began in October 1981, with full operation effective from May 1982. These sets were based at the newly upgraded depot at Laira (Plymouth), which opened in June 1981, but visited other IC125 depots for maintenance.

Unlike earlier power cars, those from No. 43153 onwards were constructed without the small guard's compartment situated in the very rear of the vehicle. Strong complaints from the National Union of Railwaymen about the inadequacies of this provision when the train was first introduced led to BR conceding that alternative guard's accommodation was needed. A second-class vehicle was designed with one less seating bay and a guard's office and luggage stowage situated in the vacant area. These Trailer Guard Seconds (TGS) (Nos 44000–101) were built in 1980 and were retrospectively allocated to each set releasing Trailer Second (TS) vehicles to form new sets.

As the economic recession deepened in the early 1980s passenger numbers began to decline. Plans to order further sets for additional routes such as North West to South East were dropped and the government's requirement that BR's InterCity sector operate without government subsidy led BR to review allocation of its precious resource. Use of IC125s on the Midland Main Line (MML) from London to Sheffield offered potential commercial and operating benefits despite the lack of 100-plus mph running. With demand on the WR declining, it was decided that some sets from this region would be employed on the MML from October 1982. Nos 253022–026 (Nos 43044–53) were transferred to Neville Hill for that purpose together with last three sets from the NE/SW allocation, Nos 253056–058 (Nos 43193–198). They were to be joined by Nos 253019–021 (Nos 43038–43) in May 1983. Although nominally designated for use on the MML, these sets were absorbed into the ER operating pool, but as seven-coach formations they were non-standard. The construction of a small batch of second-class trailers delivered in 1984 enabled the ex-WR sets to be lengthened.

A significant official change to IC125 operating procedure occurred around this time. The task of maintaining sets in fixed formations had always proved a challenge. Short-term swaps of coaches between sets to cover vehicles requiring repairs were routine, but in the main trailer formations were consistent. Keeping power cars with their allocated formation had always been more difficult. The ER/ScR unofficially abandoned this practice soon after the introduction of Class 254 sets while the WR, with varying degrees of success, maintained it. In 1984 the WR finally adopted ER practice officially separating power car and trailer maintenance cycles.

In an effort to forge a distinct identity for its premier business a new livery was adopted for InterCity traction and rolling stock in 1985. What became known as 'Executive' livery originally appeared on the small fleet of APT pre-production trains but was applied experimentally to WR sets Nos 028 and 030 along with power cars Nos 43125/126/129/130/151 in 1983. The fleet gradually acquired the new colour scheme as sets passed through Derby Works for overhaul, receiving bright red seat moquette and carpets in second class and pink and grey in first class, which replaced the old blue and orange schemes. As the 1980s progressed, in its efforts to make the InterCity sector profitable BR exploited its prime asset to the full. Examination and overhaul cycles were lengthened while spare cover was reduced to a minimum. Diagrammed mileage was maximised as turnaround times were reduced and sets were employed on fill-in turns wherever the opportunity arose. With the Advanced Passenger Train project abandoned, the 'stop-gap' train had become the backbone of the InterCity network. In the first ten years of its revenue-earning life the IC125 had exceeded the expectations of the engineers who designed it and would continue to do so for years to come.

Testing of the prototype HSDT, delayed by Union objections to the cab layout and a dispute about train crew terms and conditions, finally got underway on the Eastern and Scottish Regions in February 1973. Initially the test formation contained No. 1524, a Mark 1 RB fitted with BT5 bogies and cleared for 125 mph operation. No. 41001 is captured at York on an early test run in March 1973. (53A Models of Hull Collection, the late David R. Vickers)

No. 43002 carrying the original black and yellow livery at Crewe Works on 18 January 1976. The decision to apply the familiar blue and yellow colour scheme was taken on 15 January 1976. By this date Nos 43003/4 had also been finished in black and yellow. All were swiftly repainted, but they, along with Nos 43005/7/8, carried black infill to the InterCity 125 lettering instead of the traditional blue. (Dean Tabor)

No. W43009 captured on an early crew training run at Reading on 14 May 1976. This power car had been delivered with No. W43003 to Old Oak Common on 3 May. Delivery formations were randomly formed of the latest vehicles passed clear for traffic following initial commissioning and trial running from Derby Works. The task of forming IC125 sets into their booked formation fell to the regional home depots. (John Flowers)

Following a year in passenger service on the Western Region, the prototype HSDT was stood down. Power cars Nos W43000/1 were then united with a rake of production trailers (Nos W42010/011/014/020), loco-hauled Mark 3 No. M12140, Mark 2 FK No. 13438 and Test Car No. 6. Throughout the summer of 1976 the formation could be seen traversing the Western Region main line on trials to evaluate the impact of high-speed running on the P8 tyre profile. The unusual formation is seen here at Swindon on 24 June 1976. (Brian Morrison)

No. 252001 was drafted back into action in October 1976 on a specific diagram due to a shortage of production HST sets. Photographed on a Saturday in October 1976, it pauses at Swindon while working the 08.45 Paddington–Bristol Temple Meads. By the beginning of November 1976 there were enough production sets available to make the prototype surplus to requirements, resulting in its official withdrawal later that month. (Phil Wakely)

Power car No. W43015 leads the 10.15 Paddington to Swansea into Cardiff Central on 10 June 1977. The formation includes both restaurant (TRUK) and buffet (TRSB) vehicles. The twin catering car provision proved excessive for the Western Region's needs. In early 1978 ten combined restaurant/buffet vehicles (TRUB) were delivered to the WR, which, along with twenty additional Trailer Seconds received in 1977, allowed the WR to form Nos 253001–027 with a single catering car – ten with a TRUB and seventeen with a TRSB. The displaced TRUKs and ten surplus TRSB were transferred for use in Nos 254001–020. (John Flowers)

On 28 July 1978, No. SC43086 leads No. E43068 and the trailers of No. 254001 away from York on 16.10 Edinburgh to King's Cross. The Eastern and Scottish Regions were far more relaxed than their Western Region counterparts in keeping power cars to their allocated sets. The difference in operating practice was reflected in the gradual removal of '254' set numbers from the power car nose ends from 1980 onwards. (53A Models of Hull Collection, the late David R. Vickers)

No. 253006 approaches Reading on a Down working on 24 March 1978. This set's power cars, Nos W43012/013, were the first to be experimentally fitted with exhaust cowlings that were designed to combat the build-up of trailing exhaust deposit on cab roofs. Some power cars built towards the end of the first Class 254 batch received them from new before their fitting became standard on later builds. Their retrospective fitting to earlier power cars during works overhauls was completed in 1981. (John Woolley)

Crew training for IC125 working into Devon and Cornwall began in the autumn of 1978. Shortened formations were employed. No. W43030, with No. W43031 and three trailers, is pictured on the site of Long Rock depot, Penzance, on 7 May 1979. Opened in 1977, this single road facility with associated stabling sidings has played a significant role in conducting inspections, fuelling and 'A' examinations on sets ending their day at Penzance. (John Flowers)

The sets ordered for the West of England IC125 service, Nos 253028–040, were allocated to Old Oak Common and St Philips Marsh. With the advent of IC125 working to Devon and Cornwall, diagrams became more complex, integrating workings to and from the South West with those on the London–Bristol/South Wales service. No. W43145 from set No. 253038 waits to form the 09.30 Bristol Temple Meads to London Paddington on 5 November 1981. (Kevin Daniel)

IC125 operation on the North East–South West route began in October 1981 with a limited number of diagrams before a full service was introduced in May 1982. Cross-country sets were formed with only one Trailer First. Initially, Laira had full responsibility for the fifteen-set fleet before the allocation was shared with St Philips Marsh in 1984. On 2 July 1983, No. 43176 was pictured at Plymouth on the rear of the 10.20 Penzance to Newcastle. (Kevin Daniel)

The Locomotive Works at Derby and its sister Carriage and Wagon facility at Litchurch Lane were responsible for IC125 power car and trailer overhauls until 1988. Sets returned to works annually at the beginning of their lives, but periods between overhauls were gradually lengthened, with works visits every two years becoming the norm by the mid-1980s. This photograph shows the main workshop at Derby Locomotive Works on 10 October 1981 with four power cars in view. (Murray Lewis)

The Eastern Region was the first to adopt a policy of naming its power car fleet, with the first example, No. 43113, receiving *City of Newcastle-upon-Tyne* plates on 9 May 1983. No. 43053 was named *County of Humberside* on 10 April 1984. Two months later, on 14 June, it was still in immaculate condition when photographed at King's Cross. (Kevin Daniel)

On 10 October 1984, No. 43056 *University of Bradford* leads a Class 254 set past Ouston Junction with a train for King's Cross. In 1982/83, having dispensed with 254 set numbers, the Eastern and Scottish Regions began applying vehicle numbers below power cars' windscreens or on their nose hatch covers. (Bill Watson)

In the early 1980s the newly formed InterCity sector set about forging a fresh identity for its motive power and rolling stock. What became known as Executive livery was first applied to two Western Region sets (Nos 253028/030) and five power cars (Nos 43125/126/129/130/151) towards the end of 1983. Displaying the colour scheme on 28 April 1984, No. 43129 in set No. 253030 departs Paddington on the 10.00 service to Swansea. (Kevin Daniel)

Executive livery was applied to all power cars at overhaul from March 1985 onwards. The application of the livery to trailers was initially reserved for only those undergoing C2 (general) repairs, which included internal refurbishment. Consequently, the period of transition from BR standard blue and grey livery to Executive was protracted and it was common to see mixed livery sets during the mid-1980s. On 13 September a mixed livery Cross-Country set passes through Plawsworth with the 17.34 Newcastle to Bristol Temple Meads service. (Bill Watson)

On 26 January 1986, No. 43162 *Borough of Stevenage* leads the diverted Sundays-only 09.50 Newcastle to London King's Cross at Pelaw Junction. Close observation reveals the formation containing both TRFK and TRFB catering vehicles. This was the Heaton-based set that was confined to working the weekday diagram covering the Up and Down Tees–Tyne Pullman, which was launched in October 1985. The reinstatement of the Pullman brand offering enhanced on-board services was part of the InterCity sector's strategy to increase first-class patronage on selected peak-time services. (Bill Watson)

To increase seating capacity, ten Laira-based sets were formed with eight trailers in May 1986. On 14 May 1986, set No. 011 led by No. 43028 arrives at Reading on the 14.15 Paddington to Penzance. Conversion of the remainder of the WR internal fleet to 2+8 formation was completed in the early 1990s when additional trailers and sets were redeployed following completion of the East Coast electrification. (Kevin Daniel)

When BR decided to redeploy IC125 sets to the Midland Main Line, Neville Hill was chosen as the maintenance hub, with Bounds Green providing support, servicing sets stabled overnight in London. From October 1982 five IC125 diagrams operated on the MML, increasing to ten from May 1983 when further sets were transferred from the WR to the ER. No. 43075 is pictured passing Souldrop (near Sharnbrook) on 4 May 1987, working the 15.15 London St Pancras to Sheffield service. (Martin Loader)

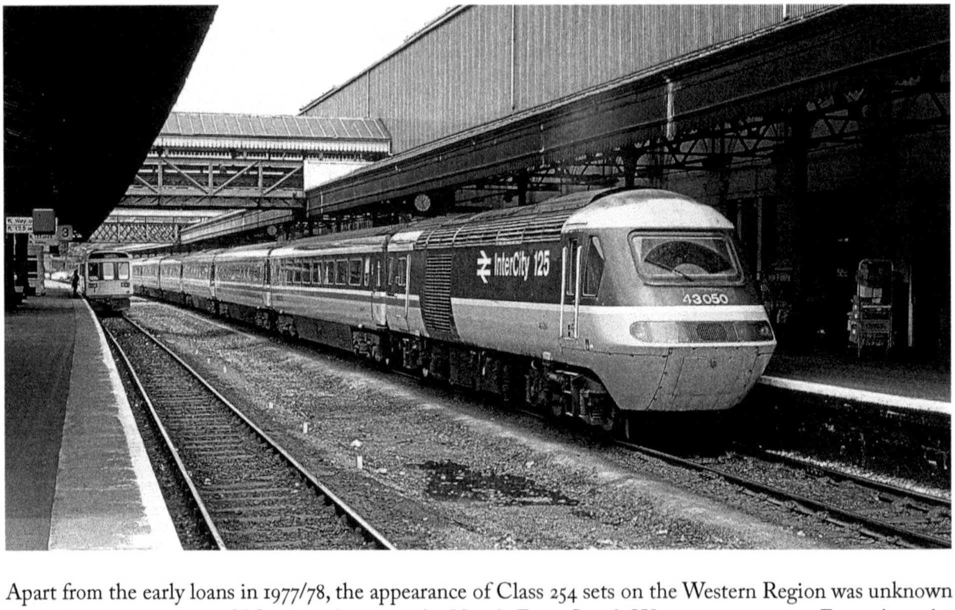

Apart from the early loans in 1977/78, the appearance of Class 254 sets on the Western Region was unknown until the inauguration of IC125 working on the North East–South West route in 1982. Even then the substitution of an Eastern Region-based set for a non-available Cross-Country set was a rarity. This changed from May 1987 when Neville Hill was given responsibility for four North East–South West diagrams. On 1 June 1987, No. 43050 heads a 254 set forming the 06.57 Newcastle to Plymouth at Exeter St Davids. (Kevin Daniel)

Chapter 2

The Train that Means Business

Changes to the structure of British Rail taking place behind the scenes were set to shape the future of the railway, and one of the most significant of these was the creation of separate business sectors each with their own identity. InterCity changed from being nothing more than a brand name into a sector of British Rail that was expected to return a profit and its fleet of IC125s was the highest-profile fleet of this flagship division. A new image was created; the livery change was subtle as carriages remained in the previous 'Executive' scheme but locomotives (including the IC125 power cars) were turned out with white lower bodysides. New italicised '*INTERCITY*' lettering and a logo featuring a flying swallow were introduced. This scheme was first applied to Nos 43051 and 43072, which operated a press launch from Euston to Milton Keynes on 30 April 1987 attached to a rebranded set. As repaints became due, the entire fleet of power cars was turned out in the new style, with the last vehicles being completed in spring 1992. To complete the new look a totally revised style of nameplate was introduced, featuring thin polished stainless steel plates matching the cast swallow logos, while most (but not all) previously named power cars received replacement plates after repaint, although sometimes after a gap of a few months or even years.

The operational efficiency and cost benefit of the fixed formation 125s resulted in plans to convert existing West Coast Main Line (WCML) locomotive-hauled trains to fixed formation operation and to apply the same system to the new electric trains that were to be ordered for the East Coast Main Line (ECML) electrification scheme. A new Driving Van Trailer (DVT) was to provide a driving cab, luggage van and guards' accommodation at one end of the train, enabling the locomotive to remain attached to the other end, resulting in shorter turnaround times along with fewer staff and movements required at terminal stations, as well as a reduction in the number of locomotives needed. A new system of data transmission using Time Division Multiplex (TDM) systems sent via lighting cables on the conventional trains was to transmit coded signals between the DVT and the locomotive.

In order to further test this system two power cars were removed from ordinary service and converted to surrogate DVTs. Nos 43014 and 43123 were chosen for this conversion and the experimental nature of the project meant they were modified by the Engineering Development Unit at Derby. Externally the modification saw the removal of the lower skirt panels and the fitting of a conventional buffer beam, allowing a locomotive to easily attach to the front of the power car if required. Internally new control equipment was located in the luggage van to create and decipher the TDM signals being transmitted through to the locomotive at the other end of the train and on the cab desk an additional control box was installed, which enabled the driver to control and monitor functions on the remote electric loco. The power cars were not intended to provide traction power, and their 415 V three-phase system was incompatible with the standard 850 V auxiliary supply on the carriages they were going to operate with, but the engines were retained, partly to act as a ballast weight and partly to allow them to be used in the event of a failure. Through Electric Train Heating (ETH) wiring was provided on both No. 43014 and No. 43123, allowing a locomotive to provide auxiliary power to the train while coupled to the power car and a Motor Alternator set was installed in the luggage van taking a supply from the train ETH to feed auxiliaries on the surrogate DVT. Testing commenced in November 1987 using No. 43123 attached to four Mark 2 carriages, and this was followed by a short period in passenger operation from December 1987 using No. 43014.

Over on the ECML the new Class 91 electric locomotives were going to be delivered around twelve months ahead of the Mark 4 carriages they were intended to operate with as a change in bogie design on the Mark 4s had delayed their construction. Eagerness to press the Class 91s into service and make use of the wires on the newly electrified route from King's Cross to Leeds resulted in the novel solution of modifying eight IC125 sets to operate with the electric locos. Six further power cars were to be modified in a similar way to Nos 43014/123 but without the need for the through ETH wiring. This work was carried out at the Stratford (East London) diesel repair shops and initially it was planned that Nos 43002–005 would be modified; in preparation, these power cars were repainted with full yellow fronts. A less ordered list comprising Nos 43013/065/067/068/080/084 were converted and these were completed during spring 1988, and they were joined in the ECML fleet by Nos 43014/123. Eight Trailer Guard Standard (TGS) vehicles were also modified with side buffers and drophead buckeye couplings replaced the fixed-head Alliance coupling allowing the electric locomotive to couple directly onto the TGS. This resulted in the fixed formation comprising a modified power car on the first-class end of the set providing Electric Train Supply (ETS) to the otherwise unmodified set and the electric loco at the other end providing all the traction power.

The first modified sets to be electrically hauled were powered by the unique Class 89 locomotive and a regular diagram on a Peterborough to King's Cross and return commuter service commenced in July 1988. The Class 89 hadn't initially been fitted with TDM equipment so always had to 'run round' in order to lead the train. The Class 91s entered passenger service in March 1989, working with the modified IC125s with only the Class 91 providing traction power. There were concerns that sustained rotation of the traction motors without power being applied would result in commutator glazing and a flashover when the motors were subsequently used. It was soon discovered that oil was being carried over into the exhaust system on constantly fast-idling power cars, which caused a couple of silencer fires. After a few weeks it was decided that the power car would also provide traction power to prevent these problems. This meant that with the hybrid electric and diesel combination some 8,730 hp was available to the train, resulting in some pretty swift acceleration! The first Mark 4 sets entered service in October 1989 and by early 1990 sufficient Mark 4 sets had entered service to allow them to take over operation of the King's Cross to Leeds services. The modified IC125 vehicles were absorbed back into normal service, although the buffers were retained on the power cars and for a short period on the modified TGS vehicles.

Electrification of the core of the ECML through to Edinburgh was completed in time for a delayed summer timetable to begin in July 1991, and part of the business case for the scheme relied upon the cascade of redundant IC125s onto other routes, where they were to supplement existing fleets or displace conventional locomotive-hauled trains. The principal beneficiary was Cross Country and, commencing from the start of the new timetable in May 1991, services including Edinburgh, Glasgow and Manchester to Bournemouth and Poole were converted to IC125 operation, bringing the type into regular operation on the Southern Region for the first time. ECML sets cascaded onto these services had one first-class coach removed, and the full kitchen catering car was not required for Cross Country operations so vehicles were swapped around, standardising the 'new' Cross Country sets to match those originally built for the route. Bogies of the Cross Country sets needed to be of the later Short Swing Link (SSL) design to allow them to operate over the third rail electrified Southern region. SSL bogies avoided the risk of the train coming into contact with the barge boards located beside the electrified rail in station areas. Other long-distance routes via the WCML, including Aberdeen to Plymouth and Glasgow to Penzance, were also turned over to 125s, resulting in significant journey time reduction. These Cross Country services had featured in the original planned IC125 route portfolio but were victims of cutbacks, which curtailed the construction programme in 1983.

Services from London Euston to Holyhead were turned over to IC125 operation from September 1991 after some shortened sets had spent the summer on the line undergoing crew training; these services used sets from the WR with sets swapping between routes every other day to return them for maintenance. The WR had received some of the displaced ECML sets to bolster their fleet to cover the Holyhead trains as well as increasing the number of their own services to cope with rising demand. Three additional sets were deployed on Midland Main Line duties, and after the cascade of the majority of sets away from the ECML a much reduced fleet was retained to operate through trains to destinations beyond the electrified sections such as Aberdeen, Inverness, Hull, Cleethorpes and Harrogate; however, later withdrawal of the direct King's Cross to Cleethorpes service, which ran from 1982 until 1993, along with improved reliability of the Class 91s saw the fleet cut still further to just twenty-one power cars to cover eight daily diagrams.

Since December 1987 the fleet had been divided into operating 'pools', which was simply a paper exercise to be able to account for the cost of running each division of the railway separately. In reality, as far as IC125 operation was concerned, any 'Western' power car could be found on the services operated by any Western Region depot, including their half of the Cross Country operation. Any 'Eastern' power car (which included ScR power cars based at Edinburgh Craigentinny) could be found on the services into King's Cross, St Pancras and later on the Craigentinny-operated Cross Country services.

In 1992 the phrase of the moment was 'Organising for Quality' as the railway prepared for privatisation with separate businesses. The effect this had on IC125 deployment was to create distinct operating pools, dedicating them to one individual route from which vehicles rarely strayed. The power car fleet at this time was split as follows:

- Ninety in pool code IWRP Great Western (including power cars nominally allocated to IWCP West Coast): Nos 43002–005, 009–012, 015–037, 040–042, 124–152, 163–177, 179, 181–183, 185–192.
- Fifty–five in pool codes ICCP and ICCS Cross Country: Nos 43006–008, 013, 014, 062, 063, 065, 067–071, 078–080, 084, 086–094, 097–103, 121–123, 153–162, 178, 180, 184, 193–198.
- Thirty–one in pool code IMLP Midland Main Line: Nos 43043–061, 064, 066, 072–077, 081–083, 085.
- Twenty–one in pool code IECP East Coast: Nos 43038, 039, 095, 096, 104–120.

A significant change in government policy during 1993 meant that instead of privatising the railway as unified business sectors, the railway was to be split, with passenger operations becoming one of twenty-five separate franchises, which became known as Train Operating Companies (TOCs), while the passenger rolling stock was to be owned by one of three Rolling Stock Leasing Companies (ROSCOs) and leased to the TOCs. The IC125 fleet was split, so the fleet allocated to Great Western and East Coast became assets of Angel Train Contracts while the fleet allocated to Cross Country and Midland Main Line became assets of Porterbrook Leasing. It should be noted that Nos 43006–008/178/184 joined the Angel Train Contracts fleet, but were 'spare', having been used as cover during the Central Door Locking installation programme; they were later temporarily seconded to the Cross Country fleet. To mark the end of the unified InterCity operation, No. 43154 was named *INTERCITY* at Paddington on 26 March 1994. On 1 April 1994 the railway was split up, with rolling stock transferring ownership to one of the ROSCOs, and the operations moved across into Train Operating Units (TOUs) ready for the franchises to be awarded. One further change was necessary to the operating pools of the IC125 fleet in May 1995, when seven of the Great Western power cars were split off into a separate fleet to operate the Euston to Holyhead services. Nos 43028/029/041/042/164–166 were reallocated to Manchester Longsight depot to operate self-contained diagrams with some infill workings between Euston and Manchester to return sets for maintenance.

With fixed formations long abandoned, Western Region still applied set numbers to the front of power cars repainted in 1987. No. 43171 arrives at Reading with the 06.18 Penzance to London Paddington on 23 October 1987 and Executive-liveried No. 43184 is visible at the rear. Note the tiny power car numbers that were standard for this livery in the early years. (Kevin Daniel)

The first two 'surrogate DVT' conversions were trialled on the WCML. The 09.40 London Euston to Birmingham New Street is seen at Coventry on 17 March 1988 with No. 43123 at the rear and No. 86240 *Bishop Eric Treacy* out of sight at the front. The Class 86 will do all the work as No. 43123 is doing nothing more than providing a driving cab. (Tony Shaw)

Eastern Region's No. 43178 has the power car number below the windscreen in the style typical of that fleet until 1992, when the numbers were omitted. The 07.50 Edinburgh to Penzance is seen arriving at Exeter St Davids on 23 May 1988, leading a standard North East–South West formation with No. 43163 at the rear. (Kevin Daniel)

Arriving at Bristol Temple Meads on 5 June 1988, working the 07.40 Plymouth to Newcastle with a set of blue/grey coaches, is No. 43147 *Red Cross*. It had been named on 3 May by HRH the Princess of Wales; the new style of nameplate didn't stand out well. Coaching stock overhaul was slower than power car repaints so mixed livery formations could be observed until 1990. (Kevin Daniel)

Buffer-fitted power cars received a version of InterCity livery with yellow around the windscreens to meet group standards. For a short period in 1988 four conventional power cars also carried this livery in anticipation of conversion. Catching the setting sun, No. 43003 approaches Circourt Bridge, Denchworth, on 22 June 1988 with the 20.00 Paddington to Swansea. (Martin Loader)

No. 43038 is seen at Neville Hill depot, Leeds, on 21 January 1990, soon after the application of this experimental livery. The white cab roof was supposed to test the effectiveness of wash plants; it rapidly became obvious that they were not capable of keeping a white cab roof clean! No. 43038's appearance remained as such until its next repaint in 1993. (Paul Corrie)

A skilful panning photographic technique using a slow shutter speed and following the train in the viewfinder resulted in this pin-sharp train against a blurred background. No. 43023 *County of Cornwall* speeds past South Stoke with the 18.45 London Paddington to Bristol Temple Meads service on 10 July 1990. (Martin Loader)

No. 43106 *Songs of Praise* leads the 'Dorset Scot' 08.40 Poole to Edinburgh on Southern metals past Worthing Junction on 29 July 1991. The scratch set has just three standard-class coaches, then a first-class coach followed by the usual buffet and a single first-class coach. Any Eastern or Scottish-based power car could be found on the Cross Country services operated by Craigentinny depot. (Martin Loader)

No. 43134 leads the ill-fated 08.30 London Paddington to Cardiff Central passing through Denchworth on 7 December 1991. Later in the journey it was involved in a serious accident inside the Severn Tunnel when the 07.00 Portsmouth to Cardiff Sprinter service formed of set No. 155306 collided with the rear of this train. Spare cabs were fabricated during power car construction so that collision repairs could be undertaken; rear power car No. 43158 received the last of these cabs, resulting in a protracted delay to the repairing of subsequent accident victims. (Martin Loader)

Just three days after it was named, No. 43020 *John Grooms* looks immaculate as it rests at Weston-super-Mare after arrival with the 11.15 from London Paddington on 28 August 1993. The rear power car was No. 43179 *Pride of Laira*. (Chris Martin)

With a freshly painted buffer beam, No. 43080 passes King's Sutton on 31 May 1994 with 1M25, the 16.16 Bournemouth to Manchester Piccadilly InterCity service. All eight of the buffer-fitted power cars joined the Cross Country fleet in 1991 and the Bournemouth route gained regular IC125 operation at this time. (Martin Loader)

The cascading of sets from the electrified ECML opened up several new IC125 routes. One of these was the North Wales coast. On 18 July 1994, No. 43192 *City of Truro* arrives at Rhyl leading the 09.05 Holyhead to London Euston with No. 43183 at the rear. The modern train contrasts with the vintage signalling equipment still in use. (Steve Vaughan)

The 12.00 London King's Cross to Inverness 'Highland Chieftain' service has just crossed the magnificent Culloden Viaduct towards the end of its eight-hour journey from London to the Highland capital. No. 43111 leads the train on 29 June 1995; the stunning landscape perfectly complements the smart InterCity Swallow livery. (Chris Hopkins)

Not everyone got the message about keeping InterCity's prime fleet looking pristine! A filthy No. 43047 *Rotherham Enterprise* is inside the original Barlow train shed at London St Pancras on 29 July 1995 after arrival on the 08.00 from Nottingham with No. 43043. (Chris Martin)

No. 43087 restarts the 07.20 Penzance to Edinburgh service from Bristol Parkway on 15 July 1996. The original Bristol Parkway station was a quite basic affair, with two platforms linked to a motley collection of pre-fabricated buildings by a basic footbridge. All buildings were replaced with more substantial facilities after hugely increased demand. (Chris Hopkins)

No. 43056 *University of Bradford* negotiates the reverse curves at Kibworth Harcourt on 25 April 1996 with the 13.33 Nottingham to London St Pancras. Although looking presentable, the white and red stripes on the front are rapidly wearing away. The 'swallow' style nameplates are barely visible in the now standard position between the cooler group and luggage van. (Martin Loader)

Nos 43163 and 43040 head west along the Great Western Main Line on 25 June 1996, en route from Old Oak Common to St Philips Marsh, Bristol. Back-to-back power car moves make an unusual sight as we have become so used to seeing a full set. (Martin Loader)

InterCity Cross Country service 1E28, the 07.04 Bristol Temple Meads to Newcastle, climbs the 1 in 37 Lickey Incline on 13 July 1996, led by No. 43103 *John Wesley*. The 2-mile bank was a real problem in the days of steam, but with 4,500 hp available, it is easy for this IC125. (Martin Loader)

No. 43004 runs alongside the Kennet & Avon Canal at Little Bedwyn on 24 August 1996 with 1C15, the 08.35 Paddington to Paignton service. This classic photographic location has since been lost to the hedge beside the fence. (Martin Loader)

No. 43028 was treated to this livery modification in the summer of 1997, with the colours of a CIE (Córas Iompair Éireann) loco being applied to the cab. The connection with CIE was that No. 43028 formed part of the fleet, working trains to connect with sailings to Dublin at Holyhead. Here, it departs Holyhead on the 13.52 to Euston on 2 August 1997 with No. 43029 at the rear. It was never known if the short-lived livery modification had official sanction. (Paul Corrie)

Chapter 3

New Looks, New Names, New Directions

The visual uniformity of the full IC125 fleet in Swallow livery was soon to be consigned to history as the new private sector owners sought to establish their identities and apply their own new liveries and logos onto their highest-profile rolling stock. The first of the five IC125 operating franchises to transfer to the private sector was Great Western, which was taken over on 4 February 1996 by a management buyout owning 51 per cent of the company; they were backed by private equity firm 3i and First Bus, who both held 24.5 per cent of the business. They promised to double the frequency of London to Bristol and Cardiff trains, although an idea to split some sets into one power car, four-coach formations with driving cabs added to sufficient trailers was soon shelved. On 30 September 1996 Great Western launched its new green and ivory livery at Bristol Temple Meads using Nos 43183 and 43185 attached to the first fully refurbished set.

Both the second and third IC125 operators to be privatised were transferred to their new owners on 28 April 1996. East Coast was taken over by Bermuda-based shipping company Sea Containers, who immediately renamed the company Great North Eastern Railway and GNER branding quickly appeared on publicity. Their new livery of dark blue with a vermillion red stripe was first applied to an electric IC225. The GNER lettering itself became the logo, although carriages wore a detailed circular crest. No. 43117 received the new scheme in November 1996 and the rest of the fleet rapidly followed: unlike other TOCs, GNER repainted their fleet as soon as possible rather than waiting for vehicles to become due for repaint. The only change to the IC125 fleet that GNER announced was a plan to extend their formations to 2+9 by the addition of another standard class TS vehicle, though the source of these vehicles became something of a saga in itself.

Midland Main Line was awarded to coach operator National Express, who announced that new DMUs would be purchased to serve intermediate stations between London and Leicester, allowing a journey time reduction on existing IC125 services to Sheffield and Nottingham. MML was to be the last operator to unveil a re-liveried IC125. The first fully refurbished set powered by Nos 43058 and 43059 was launched on 10 February 1997 and carried a new logo featuring a leaping stag, while the livery consisted of teal and grey divided by orange stripes.

The fourth IC125 operator to switch to the private sector contained the most dramatic announcements; Cross Country was awarded to Virgin Group and they declared their intention to replace the entire fleet of trains with the IC125s being usurped in 2004 by tilting DMUs. The changes to service relied on a significant increase in passenger demand to turn a £120 million annual subsidy into a £10 million a year premium over the fifteen-year franchise term. From 1998 the existing fleet was to run at least 14 per cent more train mileage and from 2002 the service was set to double, with two trains per hour on key routes. Cross Country was transferred to Virgin Trains (VT) on 5 January 1997 and in typical Virgin style a maximum publicity launch was planned for the following day on the 08.50 Edinburgh to Penzance. The first overhauled set was hurriedly repainted into the new red and grey scheme, and power cars Nos 43063 and 43068 were repainted to match.

The final IC125 operator to pass into the private sector was West Coast, which was also awarded to Virgin Group. They began operation of the route on 9 March 1997 with a promise to replace all the rolling stock, including the trio of IC125s on Holyhead to Euston services.

Initially the new companies had little scope to make changes to their fleets as the IC125s were almost fully deployed. The Edinburgh/Manchester to Waterloo services abruptly ceased on 4 January 1997, the day before Cross Country was privatised, which resulted in Nos 43006–008/178/184 becoming surplus to requirements. No. 43008 was placed into storage while the others found themselves parked at Edinburgh Craigentinny depot, just working ad hoc additional trains at weekends (and one 140 mph pantograph test run on behalf of Derby Research by Nos 43006 and 43178 on 26 February 1997) until all five joined the Great Western fleet in May. GNER reverted to a fleet of twenty-one power cars; they had been operating one additional power car since experimental VP185-engined No. 43167 joined the fleet so No. 43104 was placed into storage in late November 1996. On 12 May 1997 GNER unveiled their first refurbished IC125 set, with cast crests midway along the coach bodysides replacing the vinyl versions. Some sets from both the Great Western and GNER fleets had been overhauled into the previous InterCity style as major attention had come prior to new interior designs being created; these sets returned to works for cosmetic overhauls to bring them into line with the fully refurbished rakes. The only other power car that was not assigned to a TOC at privatisation was No. 43180, which had returned to traffic following collision repairs in October 1996 and had since been used as a short-term hire vehicle, seeing use by all four main IC125 operators.

Disaster struck on 19 September 1997 when Great Western's 10.32 Swansea to Paddington collided with an empty stone train at Southall, West London, resulting in the tragic loss of seven lives and 139 injuries. No. 43173 was leading the train and became the first production IC125 power car to be withdrawn as a result. Great Western was back in the news in March 1998 when First Group bought out the other shareholders to become sole owners of Great Western. The company was rebranded First Great Western (FGW) in December 1998. As an indirect consequence of the Southall accident it was decided that the experimental Automatic Train Protection (ATP) installation on the Great Western main lines should be brought back into regular use as much as possible. To facilitate this FGW's five non-ATP fitted power cars, Nos 43006–008/178/184, were exchanged with VT for Nos 43028/041/042/164/165, which had ATP fitted prior to them leaving Great Western to form the separate West Coast fleet in 1995.

In May 1998 VT added 43180 and one set of stock rendered surplus by MML, they also concentrated the entire fleet at Plymouth Laira depot ending the separate maintenance arrangements for parts of the fleet at Edinburgh Craigentinny and Manchester Longsight. These changes allowed an increase in the number of daily diagrams operated and when combined with marginal time extensions of existing diagrams an 18 per cent increase in train mileage was achieved. Small tweaks were made to the scope of the IC125 network in 1998. At the May timetable change VT added a Euston to Blackpool train in each direction while from September a weekday GNER Leeds to King's Cross service in each direction was extended through to Skipton. In May 1999 VT introduced a Mondays to Saturdays Blackpool to Portsmouth Harbour and return service; the whole line from Reading to Portsmouth via Guildford was new route for IC125s.

FGW finally completed the repainting of its entire power car fleet in late May 1999, but soon a new scheme was devised, which involved the application of a broad gold band surrounded by white and green bands of increasing thickness covering the lower bodyside. Fleet names on the carriages now read 'First Great Western' and the power cars simply received a gold 'First' with the circular 'f' logo. All of this was applied using vinyl over the earlier paintwork and thus could be applied very quickly. The first set to be turned out in this scheme was powered by Nos 43147 and 43172 on 9 June 1999 on the 11.45 Paddington to Bristol Temple Meads. By the end of August all sets had received the revised livery but several power cars remained to be done.

While the inquiry into the 1997 Southall accident was still underway, another far worse accident occurred on 5 October 1999. The 06.03 Cheltenham to Paddington First Great Western service collided with a Bedwyn-bound Thames Trains service at Ladbroke Grove, leading to the tragic loss of thirty-one lives. No. 43011 was completely destroyed in the disaster and this became the second production power car to be withdrawn.

At the end of 1999 the power car fleet was allocated as follows:

- Eighty–five with FGW: Nos 43002–005, 009, 010, 012, 015–028, 030–037, 040–042, 124–152, 163–165, 168–172, 174–177, 179, 181–183, 185–192.
- Fifty–seven with VT: Nos 43006–008, 013, 014, 029, 062, 063, 065, 067–071, 078–080, 084, 086–094, 097–103, 121–123, 153–162, 166, 178, 180, 184, 193–198.
- Twenty–one with GNER: Nos 43038, 039, 095, 096, 105–120, 167.
- Thirty–one with MML: Nos 43043–061, 064, 066, 072–077, 081–083, 085.
- One stored: No. 43104.
- Two withdrawn awaiting disposal: Nos 43011 and 43173.

No. 43104 returned to service on 22 April 2001 after spending over four years out of traffic. It was overhauled at Crewe and joined the VT fleet, enabling them to release ATP-fitted No. 43029 to FGW by way of replacement for the loss of accident write-offs Nos 43011 and 43173. No. 43029 had been the final power car in Swallow livery and was the first to be repainted into a new livery for FGW, which was based on the white, dark blue and pink livery applied to First Group's buses. It was unveiled on 25 July 2001 alongside one of the new Class 180 DMUs, which had been built for the extra London to Bristol/Cardiff services.

Major changes to the operating sphere of the IC125s were to begin in 2002 and this was driven by one major factor – the arrival of brand new Voyager-type DEMUs to operate all VT routes. The new trains started entering service during late 2001 and the new timetable on 30 September 2002 saw the near total conversion of all Cross Country services to the new trains, rendering some IC125 sets surplus to requirements. Ten power cars immediately left the fleet – Nos 43007/104/166/178/184 went straight to MML while Nos 43006/008 went to GNER. Nos 43013/014/062 were to leave passenger service to form a new test train to monitor the condition of the track across the high-speed routes, forming the New Measurement Train (NMT), which was operated by Serco. An all-over yellow livery was applied to the NMT, with No. 43062 being the first to wear the new colour in December 2002. The remaining forty-seven power cars were divided into two separate operating pools with VT. Seventeen sets were to remain on Cross Country duties and these were reduced to five-car formations so that they could maintain the timings of the new DEMUs. This at last allowed ten vehicles to be released to GNER so that their sets could be extended to nine-car formations some years later than previously anticipated. Flirtation with converting some redundant sleeper coaches had been abandoned due to cost and practicality constraints. The residual VT fleet was split as follows:

- Challenger sub-fleet based at Manchester Longsight and maintained by Alstom: Nos 43063, 069–071, 078, 079, 086–089, 155, 156, 159, 161, 162, 180, 193–198.
- Pioneer and WCML sub-fleet based at Plymouth Laira and maintained by Bombardier: Nos 43065, 067, 068, 080, 084, 090–094, 097–103, 121–123, 153, 154, 157, 158, 160.

It was intended that the Challenger sub-fleet would be fully overhauled and reclassified as Class 255 to operate a new Cross Country route from Paddington to Birmingham via Swindon with some extensions through to Blackpool or Manchester. Pending overhaul the Challengers operated some of these services from Birmingham northwards, but the whole scheme was dropped early in 2003 due to funding constraints, and both the Euston and Birmingham to Blackpool routes ceased in May 2003. The Pioneer sub-fleet consisted of six sets operating four long-distance Cross Country duties to cover the late delivery of the final DEMUs; this was only intended to be a very short stopgap, which in the end lasted until September 2003. WCML IC125 services were operated using four reformed Cross Country sets. The power car fleet was shared with the Pioneer pool but interworking between the two sub-fleets was very rare.

MML saw a massive change to its fleet in 2003: on 5 May a new livery of dark blue, grey and white was launched using Nos 43074 and 43166 and from 18 May a short-term service from St Pancras to Manchester via the Hope Valley commenced. Dubbed 'Project Rio', this hourly service was introduced to maintain a through service from London to Manchester while the WCML route was upgraded for new tilting trains. To operate this service MML took over the entire Challenger sub-fleet plus No. 43091 from Virgin Trains. All of these power cars required an overhaul during the period that Project Rio was operating and this itself created problems with the reliability of the temporary service, with early shortages leading to the curtailing of some off-peak services. Nos 43005/009 also came from FGW to MML; FGW was able to reduce its fleet following an increase in workings of their new Class 180 DMUs. The last day of the summer timetable on 27 September 2003 saw the end of scheduled operation of the IC125 on Virgin Cross Country, resulting in the permanent loss of the WCML north of Crewe and the Birmingham to Oxford/Reading to Bournemouth routes from the IC125 map. It also rendered eleven power cars surplus, with no other operator taking them on lease, so Nos 43090/093/099-103/154/157/158/160 were placed into storage. For some of these this was a very short-term arrangement, as by the end of the year Nos 43093/102/157/158 were back in action, supplementing the MML fleet and enabling Nos 43005/009 to be returned to Angel Trains and placed into storage. No. 43101 was moved to Neville Hill to receive an overhaul to become a fourth power car for the NMT, allowing overhauls to take place. However, it was found to be in poor condition and so was replaced by No. 43154.

In March 2004 FGW's No. 43004 swapped places with No. 43005, sending the worse condition power car into storage. Later in the year Nos 004/009 were both sent to Brush Works to be fitted with the new trial MTU engines. The end of IC125 operation on Virgin West Coast on 22 May 2004 rendered more power cars surplus to requirements. Nos 43092/094/097/098/153 remained with VT until the end of the summer to cover peak Saturday holiday trains to Newquay and then followed the others into store. Off-lease Nos 43099/102 joined GNER, and while overhauls were undertaken, Nos 43067/080 (and later Nos 43078/197) joined GNER as short-term cover. Similarly, Nos 43122/123 joined the MML fleet to maintain fleet strength during overhauls and modifications. The end of the temporary St Pancras to Manchester service in September 2004 saw Nos 43063/071/079/088/091/156/161/162/180/195 join the FGW fleet to release Class 180 DMUs to cover former Thames Trains services, which were now part of a wider FGW franchise, while Nos 43089/193 joined the general MML fleet, later to be rejoined briefly by Nos 43086/159, which returned to cover repairs.

First Group purchased twelve redundant power cars and a number of trailers in September 2004, initially as a bargaining chip during upcoming franchise negotiations but eventually to be overhauled for use on FGW routes. These power cars were Nos 43068/084/092–094/097/098/122/123/153/155/198.

On 6 November 2004 another catastrophic collision occurred when the 17.35 Paddington to Plymouth struck a car stopped on an automatic half-barrier crossing at Ufton Nervet between Reading and Newbury. The train was derailed at high speed, resulting in the tragic deaths of seven people and injuries to a further seventy. No. 43019 was leading the train, which was damaged beyond repair and became the third production power car to be withdrawn as a result. As well as the twelve First Group power cars, off-lease stored power cars at the end of 2004 were Nos 43065/067/069/070/080/087/090/100/101/103/121/158/160/194/196. Of these some had received full overhauls during Project Rio, while others were due major attention, having finished their career in Virgin livery, if not with Virgin themselves.

The ability to swap power cars between operational fleets and stored pools allowed some changes in 2005. The NMT fleet was expanded, adding a fifth power car in the shape of No. 43067 until the autumn, when it was replaced by No. 43196. Meanwhile, the completion of overhauls allowed No. 43154 to be sent back off lease. MML took back Nos 43069/086 as short-term additions until October, enabling Nos 43157/193 to go off lease in the spring while No. 43089 went off lease in the autumn. To provide summer Saturday Virgin Cross Country trains to Newquay, as well as some additional cover on GNER, Nos 43070/080/087/157/193/196 were brought back into action. In September open-access operator Cotswold Rail began leasing Nos 43070/087/157/193 to operate charter and 'spot hire' work, although Nos 43157/193 never saw passenger use with this operator.

In December it was revealed that First Group had won the franchise for the expanded 'Greater Western'. As part of the announcement, FGW was to replace the engines in the entire fleet with the new MTU units. Early in the process to bring the twelve long-term stored power cars back into traffic it was realised that the buffer-fitted examples contained non-standard wiring, so Nos 43068/084/123 were exchanged with Porterbrook for Nos 43154/158/194. New engines were also promised for the GNER power cars as part of the award of a new franchise to Sea Containers; however, it was later decided that these were also to receive the MTU engines. The 'repower' programme dominated events between 2006 and 2008 as both FGW and GNER fleets were gradually put through the process at Brush Works in Loughborough. Long-term stored power cars were returned to service as both operators took additional vehicles on lease, enabling some service expansion and allowing FGW to dispose of their unsatisfactory Class 180 DMUs. In 2006 GNER added Nos 43090/100 to the fleet, which were the first two GNER power cars to be treated. During the process the GNER fleet was renumbered as 43/2 and 200 was added to the original number. Nos 43051/053/056/057/077 joined the GNER fleet at the end of 2006 from MML to allow King's Cross to Leeds services to increase to half-hourly from May 2007. Initially these power cars continued as Valentas rather than interrupting the repower programme.

During 2006 FGW added Nos 43069/070/078/086/087/122/159/193/196/197 to their fleet and all were repowered prior to entering service. Nos 43070/087 came from Cotswold Rail after the short-term lease ended in August while No. 43196 came from NMT, where it was replaced by off-lease No. 43089. Initially Nos 43004 and 43009 were specially turned out for the launch of the Greater Western franchise in April 2006 with a vivid light blue to dark blue fade scheme broken up by bright pink, purple and white lines; a similar scheme based on a single shade of dark blue was adopted for the carriages, with overhauled power cars being turned out in plain dark blue. The repower scheme saw a significant drop in FGW reliability as overhauls and all but the most basic maintenance was halted on the Valenta engines pending vehicles being sent to Brush for overhaul. The last of the Valentas left traffic in January 2008 and the repower programme was completed in March 2008.

December 2006 saw new open-access operator Grand Central purchase Nos 43065/067/068/080/084/123 from Porterbrook; these long-term stored power cars were overhauled prior to entering service. Grand Central had been attempting to start operating open-access services since 2004. An initial scheme to operate a new trans-Pennine route through Manchester Victoria and Wakefield turned into a Sunderland to King's Cross service via the Durham coast. Delays overhauling the power cars and converting the trailers (many of which were previously loco-hauled carriages) meant that a one-train interim service didn't commence until December 2007, with the full two-train service not starting until March 2008. The fleet was turned out in a black livery. In May 2007 No. 43089 emerged, having been experimentally converted to a hybrid battery/diesel loco operating in conjunction with a specially converted TGS vehicle. Paired with No. 43160, it was demonstrated on the Great Central Railway. Once trials were over, No. 43160 was added to the FGW fleet, taking it to the planned 117 power cars.

The end of 2007 saw new franchises begin: on 11 November the franchise for the Midland Main Line was taken over by Stagecoach Group, which now included some local and regional services and was rebranded East Midlands Trains (EMT) with Stagecoach applying a blue, white and orange livery. Nos 43007/085/104/166/178/184 were sent off lease, reducing the fleet to twenty-five power cars, which were more than sufficient to operate the timetable since the delivery of new Class 222 DEMUs. The remaining seven Valenta engines were replaced with VP185 engines during 2008 using engines rendered surplus by FGW, which standardised the EMT fleet. Also, on 11 November, a revised Cross Country franchise began. This was awarded to Arriva and their plans included the reintroduction of regular IC125 operation on the North East to South West route for the first time since 2003 (although ad hoc and summer Saturday operation had continued since then). The six surplus power cars from MML joined the fleet and were back in service from May 2008. These were supplemented by long-term off-lease Nos 43101/103/121/157, which now required major overhauls. It was decided that all ten were to receive MTU engines and they were renumbered as 43/2 by adding 200 to the previous number, and the vehicles were turned out in the new sliver and dark purple livery. 12 December 2007 saw the franchise for InterCity East Coast transfer from financially troubled Sea Containers to National Express Group. The company was rebranded as National Express East Coast (NXEC) and a new white and silver livery was applied to rolling stock. In December 2008 the last NXEC power cars were going through the repower programme at Brush, which allowed them to release Nos 43053/056 off lease. These went to FGW and were also given new MTU engines in line with the rest of the fleet. No. 43089 was converted back to a standard power car following its experimental hybrid trials and it was added to the EMT fleet in February 2009. The fleet dispersal in March 2009 as the repower schemes largely concluded was:

- 119 with FGW: Nos 43002–005, 009, 010, 012, 015–018, 020–037, 040–042, 053, 056, 063, 069–071, 078, 079, 086–088, 091–094, 097, 098, 122, 124–156, 158–165, 168–172, 174–177, 179–183, 185–198.
- Thirty with NXEC: Nos 43206, 208, 238, 239, 251, 257, 277, 290, 295, 296, 299, 300, 302, 305–320, 367.
- Twenty-six with EMT: Nos 43043–050, 052, 054, 055, 058–061, 064, 066, 072–076, 081–083, 089.
- Ten with Cross Country: Nos 43207, 285, 301, 303, 304, 321, 357, 366, 378, 384.
- Six with Grand Central: Nos 43065, 067, 068, 080, 084, 123.
- Three with NMT: Nos 43013, 014, 062.

Financial problems resulted in NXEC surrendering their franchise in November 2009. This was temporarily taken over by a state-owned body known as Directly Operated Railways, who rebranded the route as simply 'East Coast' with a plain grey livery. In 2010 the Grand Central fleet followed most others and was converted to MTU engines. The fleet had been sold to Angel Trains in order to finance this and power cars were renumbered as 43/4, with 400 being added to the original number, except for No. 43123, which became No. 43423. A new station in Corby was served by some EMT IC125s and East Coast commenced a daily London to Lincoln service in each direction, partly reinstating the service lost some years earlier. From May 2011 Nos 43072/074 transferred from EMT to East Coast, replacing the ad hoc hire of one set from EMT on a daily basis. By the end of 2011 both power cars had been converted to MTU engines and renumbered to Nos 43272/274, bringing them into line with the rest of the East Coast fleet. The new East Coast franchise began on 1 March 2015; it was awarded to Stagecoach with a 10 per cent stake held by Virgin Rail holdings and the company was branded Virgin Trains East Coast (VTEC). A new style Virgin livery of red and white was unveiled and applied to the IC125 fleet from June.

On 20 September 2015 FGW was renamed Great Western Railway (GWR) with Nos 43187/188 being turned out in the new dark green livery for the launch. The 40th anniversary of the launch of IC125 services was celebrated in 2016. On 2 May an open day at St Philips Marsh depot witnessed the unveiling of No. 43002 in original livery, and an event at the National Railway Museum in York in early October saw No. 43185 returned to the popular InterCity Swallow livery. After much delay the introduction of the new Intercity Express Programme (IEP) trains to replace the IC125s on GWR and VTEC began in October 2017, allowing the first GWR sets to be cascaded to ScotRail, where plans to overhaul shortened IC125 sets to operate key long-distance services within Scotland were included in franchise plans. Nos 43021/132 were the first to leave GWR in September 2017, eventually to be followed by fifty-two further power cars.

No. 43185 *Great Western* approaches Denchworth on 1 October 1996 while operating 1C34, the 12.15 London Paddington to Bristol Temple Meads service with No. 43183 at the rear of an immaculate train. Great Western Trains had unveiled their stylish new livery the previous day at Bristol and this was the second passenger working after the 'Golden Hind' 05.15 Penzance to Paddington earlier. (Martin Loader)

No. 43063 *Maiden Voyager* sweeps around the reverse curves at Lowgill on 29 March 1997 with 1V50, the 'Cornish Scot' 08.50 Edinburgh to Penzance Virgin Cross Country service. Wearing the first Virgin livery with a yellow cab roof and 'XC' bodyside branding – later repaints received black cab roofs and omitted the Cross Country name. (Martin Loader)

No. 43096 *The Great Racer* leads the 07.50 Inverness to London King's Cross past Holme Green Crossing on 13 January 1998. GNER initially used dull gold lettering on locomotives and DVTs but changed to the white version seen here. Pictures of this style are scarce as this was soon superseded by brighter gold lettering, which remained until the company's demise. (Mick Barstow)

No. 43016 leads a Down Paddington to West of England train, arriving at Taunton on 21 June 1998. The Great Western Trains fleet was in the process of being repainted into the green and ivory livery, so matching power cars and sets was the norm by the middle of 1998. (Chris Hopkins)

Water ingress in carriage wheel bearings during late 2000 resulted in many short-formed sets, with some running with just three coaches, as depicted here with No. 43088 at Stafford, leading the 18.20 Bournemouth to Manchester on 12 December 2000. Virgin Trains had contracted maintenance of the Cross Country fleet to Bombardier Transportation ahead of them supplying and maintaining the new trains, which resulted in something of a crisis in terms of reliability of the 'old' fleet. (Peter R. T. Sharp)

One of the most famous railway locations in the country, Cockwood Harbour between Starcross and Dawlish Warren needs no introduction. On 16 July 2002 No. 43186 *Sir Francis Drake* is leading 1C44, the 14.33 Paddington to Plymouth First Great Western service with No. 43125 *Merchant Venturer* at the rear. The train wears green, white and gold stripe decals over the original Great Western Trains green and ivory livery. (Steve Vaughan)

The 08.20 Penzance to Paddington (1A45) crosses Bolitho Viaduct after its final Cornish station call at Liskeard on 18 July 2002; the train is led by No. 43152, with No. 43010 pushing at the rear. Passengers looking down into the valley will see the single-track Looe line between Liskeard and Coombe Junction. (Steve Vaughan)

Emerging from Parsons Tunnel past Smugglers Cove, No. 43029 leads 1C28, the 11.33 Paddington to Penzance, on 17 July 2002. At the rear of the train, No. 43143 is on the short open section between the Clarks and Parsons tunnels. The white, blue and pink livery with a gold band and lettering was universally known as 'Barbie' livery. (Steve Vaughan)

No. 43031 is attacking the hostile climb up Hemerdon soon after departure with the 14.35 Plymouth to London Paddington on 14 May 2003. The power car wears the initial version of the First corporate scheme; the white cab sides and front section were changed to blue on repaints from 2003. (Chris Hopkins)

By 2003, remaining Virgin Cross Country sets were reduced to 2+5 formations to maintain the same timings as the new Voyager trains, which had taken over many services. One service the IC125 still worked was the 14.13 Plymouth to York – seen crossing Blatchford Viaduct on 14 May 2003 with No. 43197 *The Railway Magazine* and No. 43086 in charge. (Chris Hopkins)

No. 43050's Valenta engine has responded as the 13.30 Nottingham to London St Pancras powers up to pass Wellingborough station on 19 May 2003. No. 43044 *Borough of Kettering* is out of sight at the rear of a set in Midland Main Line's first livery of teal and grey with tangerine bands. (Steve Vaughan)

No. 43098 *Railway Children* arrives at Plymouth leading the 11.25 Penzance to Glasgow Central on 6 September 2003. This was the last month of regular IC125 operation by Virgin Cross Country, although ad hoc hires and peak summer workings continued for the remainder of the franchise. (Chris Hopkins)

All eight buffer-fitted power cars entered the Virgin Trains fleet, and though Nos 43013 and 43014 left to form the NMT, the other six remained until the end. Showing the contrast between buffer-fitted and standard at Euston on the 6 April 2004, and with just one month of WCML service remaining, No. 43080 is waiting to work the 19.25 to Manchester with No. 43092. Meanwhile, No. 43097 will leave for Holyhead at 19.05. (John Zabernik)

During a major upgrade of the WCML, an hourly IC125 service to Manchester was operated by Midland Main Line. A dedicated fleet of former Virgin power cars were leased for the service but power cars from the core fleet frequently operated the route, as seen here. No. 43054 stands at Manchester Piccadilly waiting to work the 12.47 to London St Pancras with No. 43063 at the rear on 21 May 2004. (Gary Heelas)

Image-conscious GNER re-liveried No. 43197 for a short-term lease. Here, it is seen leading an Aberdeen service, passing Waverley Gardens between Edinburgh Waverley and Haymarket on 13 April 2005. (Chris Hopkins)

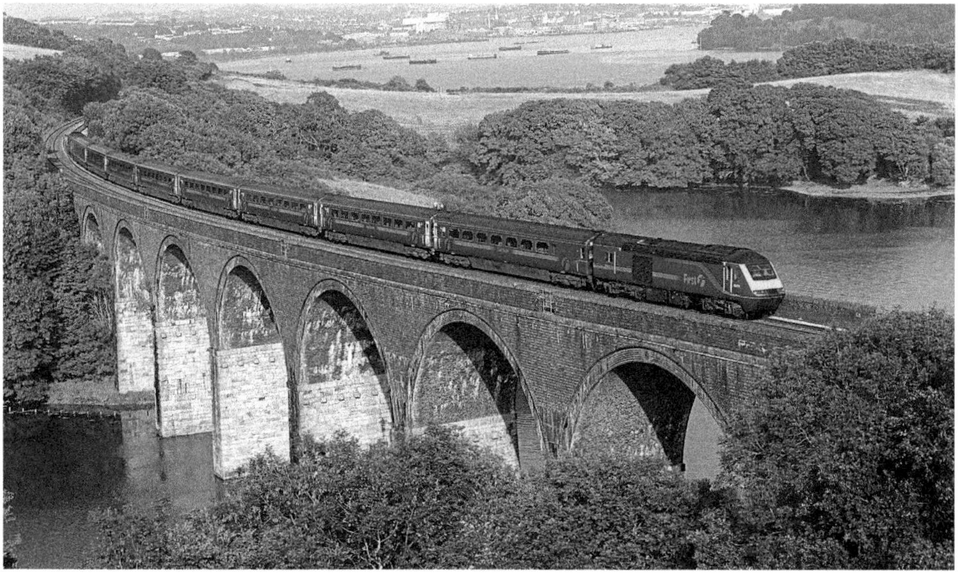

No. 43171 is leading the 15.05 London Paddington to Penzance (1C88) with No. 43162 at the rear as the train crosses Forder Viaduct on 28 June 2006. The body of water visible above the train is the Tamar and beyond is Devonport; the shipyard played a role in overhauling Valenta engines and undertaking work such as rewiring the power cars. (Steve Vaughan)

The summer of 2006 was the final year in which the original Paxman Valenta was still powering most First Great Western services. No. 43150 *Bristol Evening Post* slows as it descends Rattery for the call at Totnes with an Up Plymouth to London Paddington service in late June. (Steve Vaughan)

No. 43136 accelerates the 09.04 Penzance to London Paddington away from Exeter St Davids on 26 June 2006 (with No. 43190 at the rear). One of the batch built for the Paddington to West of England route, all the troublesome GEC traction motor-fitted power cars had by now been reallocated to Swansea Landore depot, where engineers specialised in them. (Steve Vaughan)

The summer timetables from 2004 until 2007 saw a GNER set hired by Virgin Cross Country to provide much-needed extra capacity and considerably more luggage space on key summer Saturday holiday trains. GNER's No. 43113 *The Highlands* leads a nine-coach set with No. 43096 *Stirling Castle* working 1E46, the 10.32 Paignton to Newcastle, along the sea wall between Dawlish and Dawlish Warren towards Langstone Rock on 1 July 2006. (Steve Vaughan)

1V29, the 07.24 Manchester Piccadilly to Newquay train, is also passing Langstone Rock, this time operated by a set hired from Midland Mainline. Nos 43052 and 43104 are in charge on 1 July 2006. Services to Newquay commenced IC125 operation with a special from Birmingham on 4 October 1987, which was powered by Nos 43175 and 43192. (Steve Vaughan)

Another set loaned by Midland Main Line, No. 43054 crosses the River Avon between Eckington and Defford on 15 July 2006 (with No. 43081), leading 1E47, the 09.40 Newquay to Newcastle Virgin Cross Country service. (Peter R. T. Sharp)

The 14.00 King's Cross to Aberdeen is at full speed, passing Abbots Rippon on 18 July 2006 with No. 43006 *Kingdom of Fife* leading. GNER's power cars were early recipients of modified light clusters. Each of GNERs IC125 sets were extended to nine carriages when extra TS vehicles became available in 2002, providing much-needed extra capacity. (Peter R. T. Sharp)

This unique Cotswold Rail-liveried No. 43070 is shunting out of the platform at Scarborough on 27 May 2006 having unloaded passengers off 1Z27, the 06.53 from Cam and Dursley. Four specials were operated by Cotswold Rail under their 'Heartland Rail' banner using a set powered by Nos 43087 and 43070, which were leased to save storage. (Chris Martin)

And now for something completely different! Cotswold Rail's No. 43087 certainly stood out from the crowd in this special livery advertising Hornby. On 27 July 2006, Nos 43087 and 43070 are at their regular home of Tyseley depot after arrival from Derby. The spritely performance of No. 43087 made it a favourite among enthusiasts at this time. (Tony Shaw)

On 3 April 2006, Nos 43004 and 43009 were unveiled in a new livery for First Group rail operations using large self-adhesive vinyl sheets. They ran a Paddington to Penzance special to mark the start of the new expanded franchise. No. 43194 received an experimental darker version with a purple front applied to one side at St Philips Marsh depot, while the power car was stored, pending overhaul. (Chris Martin)

Did the photographer arrange a specially shortened four-car NMT rake just so it would fit in Conwy Castle? No. 43062 *John Armitt* and No. 43013 are seen on 2 August 2007 operating 1Q24, the 09.46 Derby RTC to Derby RTC via Holyhead. Conwy Castle is a UNESCO World Heritage Site and a fine example of thirteenth-century military architecture. (Steve Vaughan)

Continued hiring of GNER sets to Virgin Cross Country in 2007 sees No. 43290 *MTU Fascination of Power* tailing 1E46, the 10.32 Paignton to Newcastle, at Clay Cross Junction with No. 43113 *The Highlands* at the front on 25 August 2007. The decal on the side is advertising Leeds to London – 'More Trains, More Often'. Expansion of the GNER IC125 fleet enabled extra trains to run. (Peter R. T. Sharp)

No. 43089 *Hayabusa* is passing Natton on 1 May 2008 while operating the New Measurement Train, undertaking track examination and recording work. With No. 43062 *John Armitt* at the rear, No. 43089 was operating attached to a specially converted coach as part of the battery hybrid trials. Although the trials were successful, No. 43089 was modified back and joined the EMT fleet. (Jack Boskett)

1S15, the 12.00 King's Cross to Inverness 'Highland Chieftain' service, is passing Blackford between Stirling and Perth on 3 May 2008. No. 43077 leads the train, having been turned out in an interim livery: white stickers had been placed over the vermillion red stripe and small National Express fleet names were later applied, indicating the new ECML franchise operator. (Martin Loader)

Cross Country acquired ten power cars and five sets of trailers in 2008 to provide extra capacity under the new Arriva franchise. Still in Midland Mainline livery, No. 43178 leads with No. 43166 at the rear of a Plymouth-bound service passing Standish Junction on 15 June 2008. (Jack Boskett)

No. 43185 *Great Western* is seen starting its journey from Cheltenham to London Paddington on 16 June 2008. The programme to re-engine the entire FGW fleet had been completed in 2007 and the fleet had a standard appearance, with power cars turned out in this plain blue livery. Taken from Cloddymore footbridge, the line nearest the photographer is the Hatherley freight loop. (Jack Boskett)

No. 43064 leads the 15.30 Nottingham to St Pancras with No. 43081 nearest the photographer at the south end of Loughborough station on 24 July 2008. The 'HST Car Stop' board helped drivers position the train correctly while calling on Up services. The East Midlands Trains franchise was awarded to Stagecoach the previous December, but this set retains the old livery scheme. (John Tattersall)

National Express-liveried No. 43277 is seen at London King's Cross on 3 January 2009 prior to departure with 1S07, 07.50 to Newcastle (No. 43311 leading). This livery was introduced by the short-lived National Express East Coast and replaced the GNER blue scheme worn by the carriages on this set. (John Tattersall)

Travelling up the stunning Settle–Carlisle line on 20 April 2009 as part of NMT duties, checking and recording the condition of the track, the 11.58 Heaton to Derby RTC via Newcastle, Carlisle, Leeds and York has No. 43014 leading with No. 43062 *John Armitt* at the rear. Each of the five coaches plays a different role in this most effective tool. (Richard Armstrong)

No. 43123 passes Gateforth on 17 June 2010, leading the 12.30 Sunderland to London King's Cross (1A62) Grand Central service. This was the original plain black livery applied to the fleet until the power cars received MTU engines; No. 43123 was to become the last operational power car with a Valenta engine. (Martin Loader)

Two First Great Western sets pass each other in Sonning Cutting on 2 August 2010. The set on the left working an Up service is a seven-coach set without a buffet car. Several sets were treated thus during the 'refresh' programme between 2006 and 2008. The Down service on the right has the long-standing eight-coach formation, with two first-class coaches followed by a buffet vehicle. (Chris Rose)

An immaculate No. 43045 stands at Doncaster while working the 13.52 Neville Hill to Hull empty coaching stock on 17 April 2011, with No. 43055 out of sight at the rear. East Midlands Trains found it profitable to use spare IC125 sets for hire to East Coast, and more recently VTEC; intensive diagramming of the high-mileage ECML fleet often resulting in a shortage of rolling stock. (John Zabernik)

The picturesque Tyne Valley line has been a regular ECML IC125 diversion over the years, and this view shows how beautiful the line can be. No. 43367 *Deltic 50 1955–2005* is seen at Bardon Mill leading the 10.00 King's Cross to Edinburgh on 21 October 2012 (with No. 43311). The train carries silver and white livery, rebranded 'East Coast' after Directly Operated Railways took over from the National Express franchise. (Bill Watson)

Temporarily wearing a red nose in support of Comic Relief, No. 43465 is 'at the blocks' of London King's Cross on 14 March 2013 prior to pushing the 16.50 Grand Central service to Sunderland (1N94). No. 43484 *Peter Fox 1942--2011* leads the train. In March 1997, No. 43068 was named *The Red Nose* in support of the same charity by Virgin Trains. (James Trebinski)

Many Anglo-Scottish IC125s now work non-stop between London King's Cross and York. No. 43239 (with No. 43309 at the rear) approaches Doncaster at speed on the 14.00 King's Cross to Aberdeen (1S22) on 20 May 2013. The power car has had grey East Coast livery applied under Directly Operated Railways management. (James Trebinski)

The route through Burnmouth and Berwick provides wonderful views of the rugged coastline. Cross Country's Nos 43301 and 43321 operate the 06.32 Dundee to Newquay past Lamerton Beach on 8 June 2013. Initially, four of the five Cross Country IC125 sets were in daily use, but this was reduced to two on most days to reduce maintenance costs. (Bill Watson)

Grand Central's IC125s served the Durham Coast line for a decade before being displaced in late 2017. On 14 April 2014, Nos 43467 and 43468 pass Dawdon with the 12.53 King's Cross to Sunderland, sporting the broad orange band along the length of the train that was applied from 2010. (Bill Watson)

With widespread depots, First Great Western sometimes has to reposition vehicles for maintenance. On 17 May 2014, No. 43150 takes a single carriage from Old Oak Common to Laira for wheelset attention, and is seen here passing Dawlish beach. The line had recently reopened after three months of repairs to massive storm damage. (James Trebinski)

Gleaming No. 43310 accelerates 1S22, the 14.00 London King's Cross to Aberdeen, from York on 9 June 2014. This was No. 43310's first operational day following a major exam and repaint into East Coast livery. The rear power car is No. 43367 *Deltic 50 1955–2005* and behind the train is the sprawling railway yard and former carriage and wagon works. (James Trebinski)

The hiring of odd power cars was common, but 8 July 2014 saw a full 2+7 Cross Country set powered by Nos 43384 and 43366 on hire to East Coast. The train worked the 06.55 Edinburgh to London King's Cross (1E04) before a run to Newark Northgate and back. It's seen beside Platform 4 after arrival from Newark and prior to returning home on the 16.30 King's Cross to Edinburgh (1S25). (James Trebinski)

The array of overhead line equipment, signal gantries, track work and signs make the approach to Manchester Piccadilly look rather complex. No. 43045 leads a full East Midlands Trains set into the terminus on 9 August 2014. It is arriving empty from Neville Hill depot in Leeds to form an additional 1Z18, the 08.45 Manchester to St Pancras, with No. 43047 leading. (Alex Wood)

No. 43206 is seen at Edinburgh Waverley on 27 March 2015 after working 1S28, 18.00 from King's Cross Virgin Train East Coast (VTEC) service. The previous plain grey East Coast livery has received a prominent diagonal Virgin band as an interim measure to obscure the previous branding ahead of full re-livery. Nos 43206 and 43309 will take the set empty to Craigentinny depot, the base for the VTEC 125 fleet. (James Trebinski)

No. 43423 *Valenta 1972–2010* speeds past Colton while working 1A69, the 17.31 Sunderland to King's Cross Grand Central service, on 10 August 2015. No. 43465 is assisting on the rear of a short five-coach set, with a declassified TF vehicle adjacent to the power car at the standard-class end. (Richard Armstrong)

No. 43163 glimpses sun while passing Uffington on 25 February 2016 with 1A13, the 10.30 Bristol Temple Meads to London Paddington GWR service. Advertising wraps significantly changed the appearance of some power cars from 2013. No. 43163 is advertising Plymouth tourism, having previously advertised Singapore Airlines. (Martin Loader)

Twenty-first-century Great Western green; No. 43187 leads the 09.00 Bristol Temple Meads to London Paddington (1A10) past Compton Beauchamp on 5 May 2016. Introduced in 2015 as a non-operator specific brand to the region's rail services, few IC125s would receive the new scheme as they were due to be displaced by new trains. (Martin Loader)

VTEC's 1S26, the 17.00 King's Cross to Edinburgh, passes Great Heck on 2 May 2016. Powered by No. 43295 (leading) and No. 43316 (trailing), the bright livery contrasts with the threating sky. (Richard Armstrong)

An open day was held at Bristol St Philips Marsh on 2 May 2016 to celebrate the 40th anniversary of the High Speed Train and of the depot that maintained them from the beginning. A huge enthusiasm for the event spread across the industry, resulting in this impressive line-up of different liveries. From left to right are: Nos 43002, 43172, 43423, 43013, 43300, 43048 and nearest the camera is No. 43187. (Steve Vaughan)

As part of the 40th anniversary celebrations, No. 43002 was transformed back to original blue/grey livery and named *Sir Kenneth Grange* after the designer of the famous cab shape. Seen on 23 February 2017, it tails the 16.02 Plymouth to Paddington as is passes Powderham. (Chris Hopkins)

Getting nearer to London at over 2 miles per minute, as IC125s have done since they were built, No. 43313 (leading) and No. 43314 (trailing) are storming towards Stevenage station while working the 07.52 Aberdeen to London King's Cross on 30 May 2017. (Chris Hopkins)

A trio of identical First Great Western-liveried power cars awaiting their next turn of duty at London Paddington on 23 June 2016, with No. 43193 nearest the camera. Paddington has been synonymous with the iconic IC125 for over forty years, but their reign will end during 2019. (Chris Hopkins)

No. 43274 *Spirit of Sunderland* rolls into the rival north-eastern city of Newcastle, leading the 17.00 London King's Cross to Edinburgh on 16 June 2017. It was given an advertising wrap and a poorly aligned nameplate to mark the introduction of a direct weekday VTEC service from Sunderland to King's Cross. (Chris Hopkins)

No. 43198 *Oxfordshire 2007* was an early recipient of the new Great Western Railway green livery and is seen passing Coalpit Heath operating a London Paddington to Bristol Temple Meads service on 10 July 2017, which had been diverted due to the rebuilding of the Bath Spa platforms for the new Class 800 hybrid multiple units. (Chris Hopkins)

Looking superb in early morning light, No. 43185 *Great Western* rounds the curve on the approach to Thingley Junction with the 06.33 Bristol Temple Meads to London Paddington (1A04) on 19 June 2017. It was re-liveried back into the popular InterCity Swallow livery scheme as part of the 40th anniversary celebrations in 2016. The cast pair of birds are original items and were provided by a collector. (Martin Loader)

'They shall not grow old, as we that are left grow old. Age shall not weary them, nor the years condemn. At the going down of the sun and in the morning we will remember them.' No. 43172 received a special livery of remembrance to those who fought in the First World War and the name *Harry Patch The Last Survivor of the Trenches*. It is seen on 12 October 2017 on the 13.05 Paddington to Plymouth. (Chris Hopkins)

Chapter 4

125s Beyond the Main Line

Although the 125s were built for pounding up and down on the highest speed InterCity routes, they have found themselves visiting an array of incongruous locations over the years. There have been many routes, interesting lines and destinations that have seen regular scheduled IC125 operation come and go, principally those lines served by Cross Country and West Coast until displacement by newer trains. Liverpool first saw an IC125 on 18 December 1981, when Nos 43175 and 43176 operated a York to Liverpool service in place of the usual locomotive-hauled train. A regular weekday service ran from May 1988 until May 1994, with the city receiving a daily Cross Country service on the main line via Runcorn. Liverpool continued to receive ad hoc substitute IC125s; most notable of these was on 21 July 1997, when Nos 43100 and 43153 on a two-coach set worked the 11.00 from Glasgow via St Helens instead of a Sprinter. This working was repeated on 9 March 1998 by Nos 43115 and 43078. Since the end of widespread Cross Country IC125 workings, the only recorded passenger workings into the city have been a couple of football specials to St Pancras operated by East Midland Trains.

Glasgow saw its first IC125 services from May 1981, when an Edinburgh to King's Cross service was extended to start at Queen Street. From May 1989 Queen Street was briefly added to the Cross Country network when The Cornishman was extended. 1990/91 timetable changes saw ECML services switched to Glasgow Central; these were almost exclusively electrics, but regular Cross Country services for the WCML brought IC125s to Central. There was a brief return to Queen Street on Saturdays from September 1995 until January 1996 when the 17.00 from King's Cross had a train swap at Edinburgh and an IC125 continued forward due to planned engineering on the line to Central.

Bradford Interchange was served by IC125s from the ECML fleet introduction in 1979 until October 1988, when InterCity services switched to Forster Square. There had been occasional diversions into Forster Square prior to this. From 1998 Bradford lost its regular IC125 service to release the set to serve Skipton instead. On 1 July 2012 Nos 43465 and 43467 worked the 10.48 King's Cross to Bradford Interchange via Brighouse and the 15.37 return as a trial run in place of the regular DMU.

January 1981 saw a daily Middlesbrough to London service begin, but this ceased in October 1982, only to be replaced from May 1983 by a Newcastle to King's Cross via Sunderland and Middlesbrough working in each direction. The Down working lasted until October 1989 and the Up working was dropped from October 1990. The route via the Durham Coast had seen diversions to ECML services from the very beginning but ten years of regular operation over the line from Sunderland to Northallerton by Grand Central began in December 2007.

Scarborough was served on summer Saturdays from 1986 until 1996 by a working from Glasgow. This was extended to Hull just for the 1991 season, enabling it to serve Filey and Bridlington.

London Waterloo was never naturally destined to see IC125 operation but the opening of the Eurostar terminal resulted in a temporary Manchester to Waterloo from May 1995 and an Edinburgh to Waterloo from July 1995. These were interim services intended to run until the introduction of through Eurostar workings, but both ceased in January 1997. The Edinburgh service initially ran via Gospel Oak but was later amended to reverse at Willesden and run via Primrose Hill. A once-daily service to Cardiff via Kensington Olympia ran from October 1994 until May 1996. Waterloo has since hosted some diverted trains; following the Southall disaster, services ran via Ascot, Staines and Hounslow on 22 September 1997. August bank holiday 2003 saw an hourly service operate via Richmond and Ascot. Four days of services into Waterloo began on 27 December 2010 when services ran via Salisbury, Basingstoke, Virginia Water and Hounslow, while Easter 2013 saw services take the direct route in from Basingstoke via Surbiton, this being repeated in December 2015. One final scheduled service is worthy of mention: namely, a Paddington to Stratford-upon-Avon via Warwick service, which ran just for the summer 1988 timetable as a trial.

Engineering work and improvements to main line routes have often resulted in IC125s diverting from their normal direct route in order to maintain a through service. While many of these diversions have been short or covered so frequently that they are not worthy of note, there have been some lines that have hosted the type covering lengthy detours or where operation has been exceptionally unusual.

Once the daily through service from London to Inverness had begun in 1984 the chance of a diversion using the Inverness to Aberdeen via Elgin line became possible. This line was a pre-planned route generally taken by the Up train on Sundays until May 1988, except in high summer. The train served all stations on the route running in the path of a local service. This line was used again just for four weekends in both directions during January 1998, but since then only one reported IC125 has worked over the line – on 13 March 2011, when Nos 43316 and 43320 operated an additional Perth to Inverness via Aberdeen following severe weather on the line via Aviemore.

Three routes from Carlisle (through Hexham, Dumfries and Ribblehead) have all seen IC125 operation at various stages over the years. Diverted ECML trains covered the line through Hexham from the very beginning in May 1978 and then for several weeks from March 1979, while a new route was built around the collapsed tunnel at Penmanshiel. While this diversion was underway a derailment at Brampton forced diverted trains to run from Carlisle to Leeds via Settle. This latter route was taken again during December 1991 in reaction to a rockfall blocking the main line. Operation of IC125s on Cross Country WCML services opened up more opportunities. The first reported IC125 workings over the G&SWR line via Dumfries took place in March 1992 and January 1993 saw diversions from Carlisle to Preston via Settle and Clitheroe. These diversions continued occasionally until 2003. One of the most unusual service train diversions took place on 18 May 1996 when Nos 43070 and 43087 operated the 07.20 Penzance to Edinburgh via Dumfries, Prestwick and Paisley.

Sunday engineering works in summer 1988 resulted in the diversion of at least one IC125-operated Plymouth to Liverpool service via Shrewsbury, Wrexham and Chester; this route was repeated by Nos 43029 and 43164 on the 08.50 Euston to Holyhead on 18 April 1997 owing to a security alert. Manchester Victoria witnessed a small number of diversions during the Cross Country era. In August 1991 some services visited while operating between Wigan and Stockport via Atherton and Denton, and a similar routing was taken up by some services in late 1998 via Bolton and Victoria.

Sleaford saw numerous IC125-operated services during weekends right from the very start of IC125 operation in 1978, but particularly during the late 1980s when the ECML was being electrified and resignalled. The ability to easily divert trains from Doncaster to Peterborough via Lincoln and Spalding would soon be lost with electric trains becoming the norm from 1991. During Easter 1993 services ran from Peterborough to Doncaster via Stamford, Loughborough and Toton instead, but the full 'joint' line saw occasional use as a diversionary route from 2008. The line from Peterborough to King's Cross via Cambridge also saw ad hoc diversions, although it was rarely used following electrification. Easter 1996 saw a weekend of IC125s passing Cambridge, and after a gap of many years the route was used again from 2009.

Various routes were used to maintain through services on the Cross Country line to Bournemouth during the IC125 era. Basingstoke to Southampton via Andover, Laverstock curve, Romsey and then via either Redbridge or Chandlers Ford was the most common way round (last reported on 28 April 2002 by Nos 43086 and 43157 on the 14.35 Poole to York), but occasional Reading to Southampton via Guildford, Havant and Eastleigh diversions were used, the first of these being in late March 1999. The Eastleigh to Havant line saw an IC125 again on 6 October 2002 when Nos 43099 and 43102 operated a diverted 12.58 Manchester to Portsmouth in place of a Voyager.

Last-minute diversions and substitutions for other rolling stock have resulted in some of the most outlandish and infrequently repeated IC125 locations. London Liverpool Street was twice visited by diverted ECML services: in April 1982 a train from Aberdeen ran via Ely and Bishops Stortford due to a strike and then on 22 November 1990 the route was repeated by a service from Newcastle following overhead line damage. When the Pope visited the UK in April 1982 three sets covered the York to Leeds via Knaresborough line to cope with demand. 19 June 1983 saw Nos 43139 and 43140 operate an Aberystwyth to Shrewsbury and return working in place of a DMU, having reached there on a special from Bristol. A DMU shortage resulted in Nos 43042 and 43155 being turned out for the 17.12 Edinburgh to North Berwick on 29 June 1987.

The Exeter to Exmouth branch has seen three IC125 visits: on 20 September 1996 Nos 43071 and 43080 operated a special from Birmingham following No. 43071's naming, which conveyed local passengers on the branch during the two runs it undertook; on 15 January 2011 Nos 43086 and 43194 operated a late evening trip to Exmouth to cope with demand from rugby fans; and on 1 May 2011 Nos 43091 and 43149 operated a Newton Abbot to Exmouth and return special to mark the 175th anniversary of the line.

The Falmouth branch has witnessed just one passenger working when Nos 43005 and 43150 worked a special 150th anniversary Sunday morning trip on 25 August 2013. Use of IC125s on the WCML into Euston created two opportunities for a set to run over the Bletchley to Bedford line. The first was on 24 January 1998 when Nos 43029 and 43042 worked the 18.43 from Bletchley and 19.25 return. On 15 January 2000 Nos 43121 and 43099 were used on the 10.35 Bletchley to Bedford owing to a lineside fire closing the main line. To cope with demand from football fans on 28 January 2012, Nos 43045 and 43059 operated a 17.34 Derby to Crewe via Stoke.

A small number of specials and charters operated during the early years. Two of the most notable of these were a Liverpool St to Southend Central via Barking and Tilbury on 1 March 1981 to mark the 125th anniversary of the line and an ambitious Paddington to King's Cross via Bristol, Leeds, Carlisle and Newcastle on 26 June 1982. It was to be the partnership between Hertfordshire Railtours (HRT) and InterCity (to operate the '125 Specials' commencing on 30 January 1988 with a St Pancras to Carlisle via Edale trip powered by Nos 43043 and 43100) that was to ultimately take the IC125 to an almost bewildering array of locations far away from the normal operating sphere. These trips were primarily aimed at the 'merrymaker' day-trip market, but a first-class dining experience became an important and profitable feature, and an additional catering car was inserted into the set for most trips between October 1989 and May 1993. The use of a precious spare IC125 was only possible during winter months when additional Saturday trains to holiday destinations were not needed. After a short break in late 1993 the specials resumed, being operated by HRT alone until the last one ran on 3 January 1998, powered by Nos 43124 and 43137, on a Paddington to Ebbw Vale and Severn Beach trip. The list of places that first saw an IC125 working one of these specials runs to a very long list, but includes Kingswear, Whitby, Ilkley, Gourock, Great Yarmouth, Eastgate, Saltburn, Lowestoft, Redmire, Cranmore, Meldon Quarry, Barnstaple, Dufftown, Kings Lynn, Pwllheli, Boulby, Rylestone, Sheringham, Falmouth, Ravenglass, Pinxton, High Marnham, Shireoaks, Workington, Wennington, Ridgmont, Bicester North, Heysham, Bishops Lydeard, Matlock, Blaenau Ffestiniog, Llandudno, Stranraer, Llandrindod Wells, Buckfastleigh and Southminster.

1997 was something of a boom year. Great Western Trains had a nationwide operating licence, so numerous tour operators emerged or started using IC125s instead of older traction, but this wasn't set to last. The inability to resource crews with route knowledge away from the normal operating sphere became far more difficult, so the very few railtours that could run did not venture far beyond the normal territory of the train operating company.

Marginal time use of IC125s from the Swansea to Paddington route included a Carmarthen to Paddington service, which was extended back to Haverfordwest in 1983 and then Milford Haven from October 1984 until May 1994. No. 43166 is at Milford Haven on 30 January 1994, having arrived on the 12.05 from Swansea, and will depart with No. 43025 leading on the 15.11 to Paddington. (Chris Martin)

1994/5 saw the final Saturday arrival at Liverpool Lime Street from Euston and the first Sunday departure to Euston operated by an IC125 to allow diversion from the electrified route. Usually running via Rainhill and often via Manchester, No. 43085 *City of Bradford* and No. 43055 *Sheffield Star* are awaiting boarding on 17 September 1995 prior to running via Warrington to Euston. (Chris Martin)

Leisure demand on summer Saturdays resulted in spare sets from London lines being used on Cross Country services. This continued into early privatisation with Midland Mainline's No. 43046 *Royal Philharmonic* and No. 43066 *Nottingham Playhouse* waiting to depart Newquay with the 14.08 to Leeds on 12 September 1998. (John Zabernik)

Portsmouth Harbour was added to the Virgin Cross Country network, and for a brief period IC125s operated the service. On 23 June 1999, No. 43153 *The English Riviera Torquay–Paignton–Brixham* is seen in 'Pompey', having arrived with No. 43097 on the 07.36 from Blackpool North. (Chris Martin)

The unmistakeable Blackpool Tower is seen behind No. 43069 as it awaits departure with the 13.06 Blackpool North to Birmingham International on 9 April 2003. Virgin Trains ran Blackpool services from May 1998 with a daily Euston service. By 2002 the town also had a Cross Country Challenger service every two hours to Birmingham. All services were withdrawn in May 2003. (Peter R. T. Sharp)

Fishguard Harbour saw IC125s from May 1986 for connections into the sailing to Rosslare, mostly in the small hours of the morning. No. 43124 (with No. 43012 at the far end) are seen at the terminus with the 09.00 from Paddington on 2 June 2002. The final IC125 to Fishguard was on 17 May 2003 when Nos 43176 and 43191 worked the 01.45 Fishguard to Paddington. (Chris Martin)

Working the 15.00 London St Pancras to Manchester Piccadilly on 9 September 2004 – the penultimate day of 'Rio' services – No. 43162 *Project Rio* leads a Midland Mainline livery set, with No. 43161 *Rio Monarch* at the rear as it passes through Edale on the Hope Valley route. A set of Rio-themed names were applied as stickers to the dedicated fleet during the final three weeks of the operation. (John Zabernik)

During the last year of operation of GNER, No. 43110 *Stirlingshire* awaits departure from Skipton on 21 May 2007 with 1A13, the 06.55 to London King's Cross, with power car No. 43008 *City of Aberdeen* at the rear. Both were still fitted with Valenta engines. The Skipton service was added in 1998 and proved to be a success, still continuing twenty years later. (John Zabernik)

During summer 2008, Cross County operated its 'new' IC125 fleet, which was still in former Midland Mainline livery. No. 43007 with No. 43184 are climbing the Luxulyan Valley, working 1V49, the 09.40 Newcastle to Newquay, on 14 June 2008. (John Zabernik)

Skegness was added to the IC125 route map from 25 May 2009 when No. 43048 *TCB Miller MBE* and No. 43055 worked the first scheduled operation to the resort starting an annual summer Saturday holidaymaker service. Two days beforehand the same set is at Skegness 'paving the way' with test run 5Z01, the 07.17 from Derby Etches Park. (John Tattersall)

Weymouth's first IC125s were an extension of a Poole to Edinburgh service for the shortened summer 1991 timetable. A one-off visit by Nos 43041 and 43124 on 23 May 2009 in place of a DMU (and limited use during the 2012 Olympics) was followed by summer Saturday services from Bristol in 2014. No. 43155 *The Red Arrows 50 Seasons of Excellence* leads No. 43195 on the 17.28 Weymouth to Bristol Temple Meads service, arriving at Maiden Newton, on 25 July 2015. (John Zabernik)

'The Pembroke Coast Express' 08.45 Paddington to Pembroke Dock service, seen after departure from Tenby with power cars Nos 43028 and 43010 on 1 August 2015. The set returned as the 14.55 Pembroke Dock to Paddington, calling all stations on the branch line. Pembroke Dock has had a summer Saturday's service worked by IC125s since 1983. (John Zabernik)

Manchester Airport has had four IC125s, the first being Nos 43078 and 43080, with two cars in place of a Sprinter, working the 06.27 from Edinburgh on 31 May 1997. No. 43078 *Golowan Festival Penzance* and No. 43070 are pictured at Manchester Airport on 8 March 2003 with 1S54, the 05.56 to Edinburgh, also in place of a Class 158 unit. (Steve Vaughan)

While stored on the West Somerset Railway following purchase from Porterbrook, First Group's Nos 43123 and 43094 were stars of the 2005 Diesel Gala. Seen at Crowcombe, No. 43123 leads while working the 13.05 Bishops Lydeard to Minehead on 7 May 2005. (Alex Wood)

Diversions can be expensive in regards to maintaining train crew competencies, but a through train is much preferred by most passengers to the alternative of a replacement bus. Diverted between Darlington and Newcastle because of planned engineering, No. 43105 is seen on the 11.00 London King's Cross to Aberdeen, trundling over the River Tees at Sunderland on 12 April 1998. (John Zabernik)

To allow major works on the Reading to Paddington route, a second round of FGW diversions into Waterloo sees No. 43012 arrived on the rear of the 08.40 from Bristol Temple Meads, with No. 43002 *Techniquest* at the front, on 1 May 2005. An hourly service via Staines was operated for three consecutive days. (Chris Martin)

Routed via Barnsley due to track relaying at South Kirby Junction, Nos 43357 and 43378 are seen at Crigglestone while working 1V66, the 11.12 Aberdeen to Birmingham New Street, on 16 May 2010 – a route occasionally used since IC125 inception. (Richard Armstrong)

Diversion of East Coast services between Newcastle and Edinburgh via Carlisle and Carstairs has become a regular annual occurrence for autumn weekends. Nos 43296 and 43308 are seen climbing Beattock at Harthorpe while working 1S11, the 10.00 London King's Cross to Edinburgh, on 7 October 2012. (John Zabernik)

A blockade at Reading for remodelling resulted in diversion of West Country IC125s from Westbury via Salisbury into Waterloo, requiring clearance to be granted for IC125s on the LSW main line between Basingstoke and Waterloo via Wimbledon thirty-five years into their operation. No. 43158 brings up the rear of 1V36, the 10.10 Waterloo to Penzance, headed by No. 43140, which is seen powering through Brookwood on 31 March 2013. (John Tattersall)

In 2015, nearly forty years after the introduction of IC125s, a 'new' London terminal, Marylebone, hosted an hourly service for two days due to Crossrail construction works, beginning from 27 December 2015. No. 43139 *Driver Stan Martin 25 June 1950–6 November 2004* and No. 43138 arrive empty coaching stock (ECS) before working the first ever passenger IC125 service from Marylebone at 09.32 to Swansea via Banbury. (John Zabernik)

Another weekend block at Reading for overhead line commissioning resulted in further diversions via the Chiltern Main Line, but for the first time IC125s were diverted via the rebuilt route through Oxford Parkway and the newly built Bicester curve. Nos 43010 and 43032 speed through Islip while working 1B51, the 14.58 London Paddington to Swansea, on 17 September 2017. (John Zabernik)

No. 43076 *BBC East Midlands Today* is viewed at the usually disused end of Morecambe station after traversing the Heysham branch on 'The Morecambe Bay Express 125 Special' 1Z37, the 08.10 from London Euston, with No. 43058 on 24 October 1992. This was the 92nd 125 Special operated by Intercity and Hertfordshire Railtours. The extra catering vehicle behind the leading TF enabled over 150 passengers to enjoy full dining. (Chris Martin)

No. 43022 prepares to depart from Norwich with No. 43187, working Hertfordshire Railtours' 1Z43, the 16.48 to Plymouth. The service would run up the Great Eastern Main Line via Ipswich, Colchester and Stratford, and then the North London Line via Primrose Hill and Acton Wells Junction on 15 June 1996. (John Zabernik)

Great Western's No. 43012 (with No. 43185 *Great Western*) at London Liverpool Street on 29 June 1997 with Hertfordshire Railtours' 'The Arch Weaver' 1Z72, the 09.30 to Waterloo. This mystery excursion took in visits to Southminster and Southend Victoria before traversing the North London Line, Gospel Oak and Kensington Olympia. (John Zabernik)

The Cotswold Line Promotion Group chartered a GW IC125 for their annual excursion from 2009 to 2017. No. 43139 *Driver Stan Martin 25 June 1950–6 November 2004* and No. 43151 await departure from resignalled and remodelled Scarborough on 15 September 2012 with 'The Cotswold–Ouse Express' return 1Z35, 16.15 to York, continuing as 1Z45, the 17.22 York to Oxford via Birmingham, Worcester Shrub Hill and Cotswold line stations. (Tony Shaw)

From 2011 EMT operated occasional trips, mostly as charity specials, taking IC125s onto preserved lines. Some were marketed by UK Railtours and destinations have so far included Dereham, Oxenhope, Rawtenstall, Wansford, Rowsley and Swanage. 'The Pickering Paxman' on 15 July 2017, seen here, was also run. This was a joint EMT, Branch Line Society and 125 Group venture from Derby to Pickering and Whitby in aid of the charity Railway Children, shown by the headboard displayed on No. 43082 *Railway Children* at Grosmont. No. 43044 brings up the rear. (John Zabernik)

About as far away from the UK main line as it's possible to go! The eXpress Passenger Train (XPT) was British Rail's only IC125 export. Built in Australia by Comeng from 1981 to 1985, and topped up in 1991, the fleet consists of nineteen power cars (Nos XP2000–XP2018), which were originally fitted with Valentas but were converted to VP185s from 2000 to 2002. Power output is 2,000 hp with a maximum speed of 100 mph and there are sixty passenger vehicles in the fleet. No. XP2005 leads No. XP2015 at Strathfield, working the 14.10 Dubbo to Sydney on 2 December 2009. (John Zabernik)

XPTs typically run in 2+5 formation, operating services radiating from Sydney (where they are maintained) to Melbourne (approximately eleven hours, 597 miles), Dubbo (six hours, 287 miles) and over the North Coast Main Line to Grafton, Casino and Brisbane (fourteen hours, 613 miles). A shorter four-coach rake provides a daily return service from Sydney to Dubbo. On 1 April 2017 this was powered by Nos XP2009 and XP2007, which are seen at Dubbo after arriving on WT27, the 07.18 from Sydney. (John Tattersall)

Chapter 5

Valenta, a Tough Act to Follow

BR had put a lot of time and effort in getting the Valenta to perform well in the IC125. In particular, during the early 1980s they started exchanging the original fabricated engine blocks in preference for cast blocks to make the engines more resilient to the demands of thermal cycling. But after problems with failing exhaust manifolds in the summers of 1983 and 1985, BR decided they would start looking for a replacement engine.

BR went to four manufactures – Mirrlees Blackstone, Pielstick, MTU and Paxman – asking for a suitable replacement engine, and after due consideration the Mirrlees MB190 engine was selected. The new engine was a 90 degree V (against the Valenta 60 degree) twelve-cylinder unit with a capacity of 71.5 litres against the Valenta's 79 litres. With electronic Heinzmann engine governing, the power unit offered considerable fuel, saving over the Valenta and also improving reliability.

No. 43091 was used to test clearances at Derby during 1986 and, after much deliberation by BR about where to base the reworked power cars, Nos 43167–170 were chosen as the test candidates. After installation during 1987 the power cars worked on the Western Region with a good level of availability, albeit with one early problem when No. 43169 caught fire. BR had opted to rate the engine at its stated 2,400-hp rating, which was too much for the traction rectifiers. All power cars were then reduced to 2,250 hp as per the Valenta.

Although the experiment was on the surface successful, two of the power cars, Nos 43167 and 43170, were stood down in February 1992 and November 1991 respectively to provide parts to keep Nos 43168 and 43169 going. BR could not get the service commitment they wanted or needed from Mirrlees and effectively the experiment was dead, albeit with the two remaining power cars soldiering on.

At around the same time as the two Mirrlees power cars were stood down, Paxman had started developing a new engine. The VP185 was a ground-up design that shared only ancillary part commonality with the Valenta. The engine was way ahead of its time with two-stage turbocharging (using a staggering six automotive turbochargers), electronic engine governing and unit injector fuel pumps. Measuring 65 litres in swept volume across its twelve cylinders and with a 90 degree V, it was much more compact than the Valenta. BR decided to re-engine redundant No. 43170 with the new engine type, and with much work at Plymouth Laira the power car was released into traffic in 1994.

Initial indications were that the engine provided good fuel economy and reliability, running with Valenta-fitted No. 43143 for much of the time for comparison. BR then placed an order for three more engines, which were fitted to Nos 43169 and 43168, as well as to No. 43167, which itself was transferred to East Coast for trials on the Anglo-Scottish route. This work was completed at Crewe Works due to the amount of mechanical work required.

With the trials on the Western continuing, Porterbrook Leasing decided to fit four of their power cars with the engine type for testing on the Midland Main Line. Nos 43047 and 43075 were fitted in the late autumn of 1995 at Neville Hill depot in Leeds, although not without issues; No. 43047 suffered a runaway engine during early testing and both suffered from slow power delivery problems. So much was the concern that the fitting of the remaining two engines was paused while work by the engine manufacturer was carried out. Then, in late 1996, Nos 43059 and 43074 were converted to VP185 and the trials continued, while Great Western added a further four VP185 power units to their fleet in 1997 when Nos 43173/177/179/191 were converted.

Overall Porterbrook and MML were happy with the engine type and decided that with some further work between themselves, Paxman and Brush Traction at Loughborough the engine type would be a suitable engine for the IC125. The reason Porterbrook wanted to re-engine was due to the diminishing number of Valenta blocks, especially with the recessed deck variety that were prone to coolant leaks, and fitting the new engine type would provide a welcome surplus of the more reliable flat-top engines. A contract was placed with DML at Devonport to rewire and re-engine fourteen power cars in the fleet between March 2002 and February 2004, with the power cars being moved to Devonport by road from Derby Etches Park.

Angel Trains, meanwhile, had put a lot of time and effort into looking at re-engineering power cars with the MTU V4000 R41 engine, which was a compact sixteen-cylinder unit from Germany. First Great Western had never been completely happy with their VP185 fleet so two power cars, Nos 43004 and 43009, were fitted with the new engine type and a 'shoot out' between VP185 and MTU took place on the Western Region. In the end the MTU engine was chosen, initially as a twenty-six power car conversion contract. The engine was deemed so successful that the entire FGW fleet was to then be repowered with the German prime mover, which is a modern electronically monitored engine for the twenty-first century and is afforded a level of maintenance attention that was not lavished on previous power car engines.

With FGW repowering their entire fleet to MTU, the opportunity was taken by Porterbrook to acquire the surplus VP185 engines and fit them to the remaining power cars on the Midland Main Line that still had original Valenta engines fitted, giving the operator a common engine type on all their power cars.

The decision to repower the whole Western fleet marked the end for the Valenta as GNER, followed by Cross Country, Network Rail and finally Grand Central, all converted their power cars over to MTU. The final Valenta-fitted production power car was No. 43123, which was eventually switched off on 23 December 2010, bringing an end to over thirty years and hundreds of millions of miles of service by the trusty Valenta.

A Mirrlees MB190 diesel engine attached to a Brush BA1001B alternator at Derby Locomotive Works in autumn 1986, awaiting fitment. The mounting arrangement is quite different to the original Paxman Valenta, requiring extensive bedplate steelwork to locate the engine. (Doug Harvey)

No. 43167 sits 'on the blocks' at London Paddington on 31 January 1987, having been recently out-shopped from Derby Locomotive Works with a Mirrlees MB190 engine and new Serck Behr cooler group. The power car is plugged into the shore supply to allow a 415 V three-phase mains feed for the carriage auxiliaries and battery chargers with both engines shut down. (Kevin Daniel)

An overhauled Paxman VP185 engine attached to a Brush BA1001B alternator is lowered into No. 43082 *Railway Children* at Neville Hill depot during an engine change on 4 June 2013. The major difference to the Valenta and MB190 types was the use of six automotive-type turbochargers contained in cassettes above the V of the engine. The starter motor was also moved to the opposite side from a Valenta engine. (James Trebinski)

No. 43167 at King's Cross on 16 January 1996, having arrived with the 09.55 from Aberdeen on its second day working as a VP185-engined machine. This power car proved popular with drivers for its startling performance, which was later found to be a wrongly adjusted governor. In order to simplify GNER power car maintenance, No. 43167 lost its non-standard VP185 engine in favour of a Valenta during summer 2001. This in turn allowed FGW to convert No. 43165 into a VP185. (Chris Martin)

Pristine No. 43048 at St Pancras on 25 May 2004 with the 14.30 from Nottingham. No. 43048 was the first to receive the full electronics upgrade from Brush Traction, which involved the replacement of 1970s thyristor technology with twenty-first century MOSFET and FPGA devices and a new Knorr Bremse wheel slide system using dedicated axle probes rather than the unreliable traction motor probes used previously. The power car remains one of only two in the EMT fleet (with No. 43089) that carry upgraded data monitoring capability, and which act as test beds for any new technology. (Tony Shaw)

'Heavy General Overhaul' is the term British Rail would have used. Traction re-engineering is how they described the work undertaken by Brush Traction to the power cars fitted with MTU 16V4000 engines. No. 43181 *Devonport Royal Dockyard 1693–1993* is seen during October 2007, having been stripped of most components and being moved from one shop to another for 'rebuilding'. The work included the installation of the MTU engine and the installation of a new cooler group, as well as, in some cases, rewiring and body rectification work. (John Tattersall)

The first completed production power car MTU repower at Brush, No. 43175, stands outside the works in a temporary livery involving all the project stakeholders – owner Angel Trains, operator First Group, contractor Brush and engine manufacturer MTU. No. 43175 was released from the works in the now common plain blue livery. (Stuart Maclean)

MTU 16V4000 R41 diesel engine 3005 attached to a Brush BA1001C alternator outside the MTU East Grinstead factory on 23 October 2015. Being unique among power car engines at sixteen cylinders, installation in the engine room is tight. This was the first East Coast MTU to receive a QL4 overhaul in Germany and was painted in Virgin red. Chrome rocker covers were added by MTU. (Peter Starks)

The last two re-power cars for FGW go through the final stages of test and paint at Brush. On the left is No. 43253 (No. 43053) and on the right is No. 43056, waiting to be repainted. These power cars are unique in the FGW fleet, having upgraded Brush electronics, which were fitted during their time with MML. Removing the equipment would have been a retrograde step, so initially a plan was made to renumber them to the 4325x range. This was never sanctioned and No. 43253 reverted to No. 43053 instead. (Stuart Maclean)

No. 43089 *Hayabusa* had an interesting interlude to its career when it was converted to become a hybrid power car. The project saw the DC motors being replaced by AC motors and redundant TGS No. 44062 being converted into a battery coach. Using sophisticated electronics the power car used battery power at slow speed and then blended diesel power as it accelerated. It also harvested energy under braking to recharge the batteries. No. 43089 and unmodified No. 43160 *Porterbrook* are seen stabled at Quorn and Woodhouse on 3 June 2007 during trials on the Great Central Railway. (Steve Vaughan)

Chapter 6

Project Miller; Prototype Metamorphosis

125 Group was formed in 1994 by a small group of enthusiasts to provide a focus point for information and news regarding the HST. Since then it has grown into a preservation organisation with over 500 members, having restored and now operating the prototype HSDT power car No. 41001, owning and operating six Mark 3 coaches and is still providing a high-quality quarterly magazine. But how did it get to operate the prototype power car long before any production power car? This chapter tells that story.

The sole remaining prototype power car, No. 41001, had long been a static exhibit at the National Railway Museum in York. Its sister power car, No. 41002, had been scrapped in 1990 and the coaches disbanded to find new roles in passenger traffic, as test vehicles or in the Royal Train. 125 Group had attended several events at York and we were pondering what to do, given that at the time IC125 preservation was still some way off, and we were at risk of losing momentum. It was agreed that we would approach the NRM with a view to restoring No. 41001 to operational condition. There was one significant enabler to the idea in that the museum had been donated a Paxman Valenta engine (S508) from No. 43143 during the MTU re-power programme. No. 41001 then had a sectioned engine, which had made many attempts to resurrect it before unattainable. 125 Group produced a detailed inspection report of the power car and after some detailed and lengthy negotiations Project Miller was born.

Why Project Miller? It was a way of giving the venture its own identity and was also outside of our then core objectives. The name was a relatively easy one to think of: Terry Miller was instrumental in the birth of the High Speed Train concept and as such the prototype was really his baby. Miller began as an apprentice under Sir Nigel Gresley and ended up as Chief Engineer (Traction and Rolling Stock) for British Rail in 1968. It seemed only fitting that we name the project after him.

Then came the problem of where to do the work. Fortunately, our friends at East Midlands Trains came to the rescue with a kind offer of space at Neville Hill depot in Leeds, a depot linked with IC125s since their introduction and also the home depot of No. 41001 during its initial testing in 1972. The move to Neville Hill was not without logistical problems as No. 41001 had not been moved for several years, and as such would have to be un-braked. Using a number of coaches as brake force runners, No. 41001, hauled by No. 31601, made a historic move on 29 March 2012. The move went without any issues and we were greeted by an enthusiastic crowd at Neville Hill and welcomed to the depot.

Our first task was to reinstate brakes on the vehicle as we had a prior engagement with No. 41001 being required for Railfest at York during May. No time was wasted putting air onto the power car and to our astonishment the brakes still worked! It is a testament to the quality of the parts BR used to use from Davies & Metcalfe and Westinghouse that the seals on the various valves and pipes were mainly leak free. Next we would need the main air reservoir tanks overhauled as these were long since out of certification. Wabtec came to rescue and offered to do the tanks for us at Loughborough with a quick turnaround so we could reattach the tanks before No. 41001 moved back to York for the Railfest.

Railfest itself was the first opportunity we had to show off No. 41001 to the public properly, with the cab and van area all open so people could see the task we had in front of us and to raise some welcome money to fund the exercise. Getting to York was far simpler given we now had working brakes, with No. 55022 hauling us the short distance from Leeds. First Great Western had also joined in the fun by temporarily covering No. 42353 in a prototype vinyl livery to match No. 41001, as well as sending speed record holder No. 43159 to show alongside. 125 Group was entrusted with manning all the vehicles through the week-long venture, and there was a huge amount of interest in our fledgling project.

After Railfest we moved back to Neville Hill and settled into the core of the work. First on the agenda was swapping the engines over. 125 Group had already done significant work on S508 at its own facility before delivering it to Leeds. EMT were excellent in assisting with the roof and power unit removal, splitting the alternator from the sectioned engine and then mating it to the replacement. Installation was without issue so we now had a power car that would actually do something useful, but we were a long way from the finish line as we had two major issues: electrics and brake pads.

We initially thought we could make the wiring work but decided we needed to rewire at least the cubicle, which was removed during the engine change and then stripped, painted, rebuilt and rewired over a period of several months. Hindsight is a wonderful thing: in the final analysis we found we have actually rewired 80 per cent of the power car, such was the state of the wiring as we moved from system to system.

The other main issue was brake pads; those on No. 41001 were over thirty years old and impregnated with asbestos. We really needed to change them to avoid any failure of the ageing material so we approached several manufacturers until Becorit came to the rescue. As the power car had original Girling brake rigging rather than BSI, which the power cars now have, the pads are no longer manufactured, so the blank pads were sent to Germany and then refaced by hand in their laboratory. The result was excellent and as of 2017 we are still using these pads, which have only marginally worn; BSI brake rigging will be a future project in itself!

The day came to start up the engine but this was somewhat problematic. Much of the press had turned up and we had not done any real prep work due to time constraints. After much turning over the press left, along with most depot staff, but undeterred we thought of old diesel preservation techniques for reviving old engines. We removed the injectors, cleaned them, put some oil down the bores, refitted and went for start – success! The engine coughed and spluttered into life. We'd done it; but now we needed to make it move on its own.

EMT were under pressure for space and, not wanting to outstay our welcome, we started looking for a permanent home. We finally settled on the Great Central Railway Nottingham (GCRN) and during September 2013 said a fond farewell to our hosts as we moved to pastures new. However, before we left we arranged for No. 41001 to receive a new coat of paint using the paint booth facilities at Neville Hill and the skill of the A1 Pro-Paint team. As they used the latest paint process we were confident the power car would survive many winters in the UK without substantial degradation.

We left Leeds knowing that we had a hill to climb as it had turned out that No. 41001 had been left with an original style alternator, and not the production style setup with three-phase electric train supply (ETS). We would need to change the setup so that we could produce 110 V from the auxiliary alternator, with 850 V from the ETS alternator as a by-product, and then drive the relatively low impedance drive of the main alternator.

Dave Moore from Brush at Loughborough came to the rescue and after a long discussion we narrowed down the solutions to two; either fit a Heavy General Refurbishment Class 37 electronics kit, albeit with the governor modified to work with the load regulator, or fit a Class 57 electronics rack and separate Automatic Voltage Regulator (AVR). The latter was the preferred option, but where would we find a Class 57 rack? Fortunately, Dave had spotted one at Brush that was built but never used in a locomotive, and we were granted permission to use it in No. 41001.

To finish the electronics puzzle we also had to fit an AVR to control the 110 V battery charge and ETS. We decided we should buy a new unit from Noel Craigen, who had fitted many of his solid state MOSFET drive units to Class 47s at Tinsley during his time there and also now to a large number of preserved locomotives.

With both of these fitted, and some static testing, a historic moment occurred on 31 May 2014 when No. 41001 took power for the first time in over twenty-seven years. It had been a herculean effort by all involved, but the results were superb. Project Miller – project complete!

Where it all started. No. 41001 is seen sitting in *The Great Hall* at the National Railway Museum in York on 21 September 2004. The power car had not worked in over twenty years and was rarely open to the public; however, having been kept mostly undercover, the bodywork condition was, for the most part, excellent. (John Tattersall)

The first job on arrival at Neville Hill was to get the braking system working, and the most important item to address was the air reservoir tanks. No. 41001 put up a good fight but we eventually wrestled them off so they could be sent away for overhaul and recertification at Brush, Loughborough, who kindly did the work for free as one of our project sponsors. The triumphant team pose with the air tanks on the floor of the Back Fitting Shop at Neville Hill, Leeds, on 26 March 2012. (John Zabernik)

With a working braking system – note the new brake hoses – No. 41001 proudly stands at Railfest, which was a week-long event held by the National Railway Museum in York during early June 2012. This was the first opportunity we had to really show off No. 41001 to the public and explain what work was required. Over 1,000 people visited the cab for a short talk by our volunteers. FGW supported the event by sending world speed record holder No. 43159 and prototype TS No. 42353, which they had temporarily wrapped in a prototype livery to match No. 41001. (John Tattersall)

Returning to Neville Hill, the major task of replacing the sectioned Valenta engine with a functioning one got underway. Valenta S508, last used in power car No. 43143, is mated to the prototype alternator set at Neville Hill on 28 June 2012. Fortunately, the depot had kept both the original Valenta engine stand and lifting beam, making the exercise much easier. The engine had been prepared by 125 Group at its own facility prior to its installation in No. 41001. (Alex Wood)

Valenta engine S478 undergoing testing at Paxman Diesel's factory in Colchester on 20 March 2007 after receiving some rectification work at the facility. The test house can run engines at full main alternator loading for extended periods to check for problems before dispatching to the customer. This engine ended up being the last Valenta fitted to No. 43104 and is now in storage as part of 125 Group's long-term pool of Valentas. The governor from this engine is now fitted to S508, which is inside No. 41001. (John Tattersall)

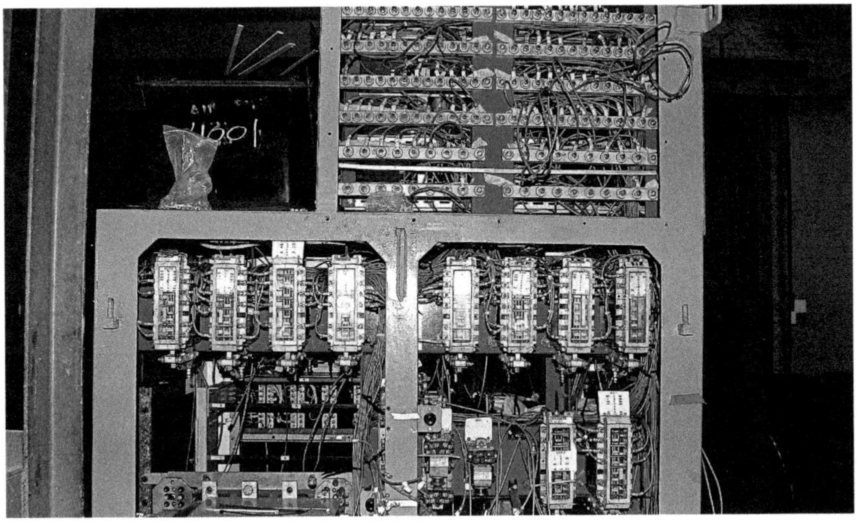

Another major task was rewiring the power car. This started with a strip and rebuild of the electrical cubicle, which was easier when removed from the power car. Once emptied, the cubicle was repainted, with the internals being coated in anti-tracking paint, and then overhauled relays and contactors were installed. Rewiring was a painstaking task, taking many months and requiring hundreds of wires to be connected together. The terminal rails at the top of the unit are used to connect the cubicle (fundamentally the brain of the power car) to the rest of the vehicle. (Tony Shaw)

After much hard work, S508 erupts into life outside the Back Fitting Shop at Neville Hill on 1 July 2013. The day had been fairly fraught with us trying to get the engine started, but fortunately some old preservation 'tricks of the trade' saw us pour a little oil down each cylinder bore and to clean the injectors, which led to the engine starting during early evening. Note the bodywork, which has been rubbed down ready for repainting. (Tony Shaw)

A fine illustration of No. 41001 posing outside the Back Fitting Shop at Neville Hill on 16 August 2013 after a full repaint by A1 Pro-Paint in their paint booth. Using a spray paint system, it has already seen No. 41001 through several winters of British weather. Given a good clean, it always looks immaculate. (Paul Corrie)

Testing, testing. Once we had all the electrical system connected and statically tested, the next step was a test run. On 31 May 2014, No. 41001 was hooked up to some Mark 2 coaches and No. 56097 for its first tentative steps on the Great Central Railway (Nottingham) GCRN. Here, No. 41001 awaits the first application of power at Fifty Steps. The test run was extremely successful, with only a couple of minor running faults noted. A second test run later in the summer showed it was fit to enter passenger traffic. (John Zabernik)

Project completed! On 15 November 2014, after several years of hard work, 125 Group celebrated the launch of No. 41001 as an operational power car with EMT kindly providing a mini IC125 set. *The Screaming Valenta* started in Derby, conveying invited guests as well as fare-paying members to Ruddington, where No. 41001 was attached to the train for a return run down the line. The day was a huge success and was attended by many of those involved with running the IC125 on a day-to-day basis from around the country. Here, the 125 Group team pose in front of No. 41001 along with Honorary President Sir Kenneth Grange, Tim Shoveller (who originally authorised us going to Neville Hill) and David Horne (then managing director of EMT). (Tony Shaw)

Doing its day job: No. 41001 is hard at work on the GCRN at Barnstone Sidings on 21 February 2016. 125 Group decided to purchase three loco-hauled Mark 3 coaches (Nos 11074, 10206 and 12092) to complement No. 41001, and this was the first run with the coaches after they had received a full repaint into matching prototype livery by Wabtec Scotland at Kilmarnock. (James Trebinski)

Out and about. 2016 saw 125 Group tour the country with No. 41001 and its Mark 3 coaches, with the Mid Norfolk Diesel Gala being one of the highlights. Hauling five Mark 3 coaches and Peak No. 45133, No. 41001 opens up to Notch 5, passing Hardingham station with a photo special on 1 April 2016. No. 41001 also visited the Nene Valley Railway and had its first trip to Scotland in preservation for the Bo'ness Summer Diesel Gala. (John Tattersall)